SCHIZOPHRENIA

LOSING TOUCH WITH REALITY

Anorexia Nervosa:
Starving for Attention

Child Abuse and Neglect:
Examining the Psychological Components

Conduct Unbecoming:
Hyperactivity, Attention Deficit, and Disruptive Behavior Disorders

Cutting the Pain Away:
Understanding Self-Mutilation

Drowning Our Sorrows:
Psychological Effects of Alcohol Abuse

Life Out of Focus:
Alzheimer's Disease and Related Disorders

The Mental Effects of Heroin

Psychological Disorders Related to Designer Drugs

Psychological Effects of Cocaine and Crack Addiction

Schizophrenia:
Losing Touch with Reality

Sibling Rivalry:
Relational Disorders Involving Brothers and Sisters

Smoke Screen:
Psychological Disorders Related to Nicotine Use

Through a Glass Darkly:
The Psychological Effects of Marijuana and Hashish

The Tortured Mind:
The Many Faces of Manic Depression

When Families Fail:
Psychological Disorders Caused by Parent-Child Relational Problems

A World Upside Down and Backwards:
Reading and Learning Disorders

THE ENCYCLOPEDIA OF PSYCHOLOGICAL DISORDERS

Senior Consulting Editor Carol C. Nadelson, M.D.
Consulting Editor Claire E. Reinburg

SCHIZOPHRENIA
LOSING TOUCH WITH REALITY

Daniel E. Harmon

CHELSEA HOUSE PUBLISHERS
Philadelphia

The ENCYCLOPEDIA OF PSYCHOLOGICAL DISORDERS provides up-to-date information on the history of, causes and effects of, and treatment and therapies for problems affecting the human mind. The titles in this series are not intended to take the place of the professional advice of a psychiatrist or mental health care professional.

Chelsea House Publishers
Editor in Chief: Stephen Reginald
Managing Editor: James D. Gallagher
Production Manager: Pamela Loos
Art Director: Sara Davis
Director of Photography: Judy L. Hasday
Senior Production Editor: LeeAnne Gelletly

Staff for SCHIZOPHRENIA: LOSING TOUCH WITH REALITY
Prepared by P. M. Gordon Associates
Associate Art Director: Takeshi Takahashi
Cover Designer: Brian Wible

The Chelsea House World Wide Web site address is
http://www.chelseahouse.com

First Printing

9 8 7 6 5 4 3 2 1

Library of Congress Cataloging-in-Publication Data applied for

ISBN 0-7910-4953-1

CONTENTS

Introduction by Carol C. Nadelson, M.D.   6

Overview: Schizophrenia   9

1   Where Do I Find the Real World?   13

2   Understanding Schizophrenia   23

3   Diagnosis   35

4   Effects on Caregivers and Society   47

5   What Causes Schizophrenia?   53

6   Treatment and Care   65

7   The Future—and How You Can Help   75

Appendix: For More Information   82

Bibliography   84

Further Reading   86

Glossary   88

Index   90

PSYCHOLOGICAL DISORDERS AND THEIR EFFECT

CAROL C. NADELSON, M.D.
PRESIDENT AND CHIEF EXECUTIVE OFFICER,
The American Psychiatric Press

There are a wide range of problems that are considered psychological disorders, including mental and emotional disorders, problems related to alcohol and drug abuse, and some diseases that cause both emotional and physical symptoms. Psychological disorders often begin in early childhood, but during adolescence we see a sharp increase in the number of people affected by these disorders. It has been estimated that about 20 percent of the U.S. population will have some form of mental disorder sometime during their lifetime. Some psychological disorders appear following severe stress or trauma. Others appear to occur more often in some families and may have a genetic or inherited component. Still other disorders do not seem to be connected to any cause we can yet identify. There has been a great deal of attention paid to learning about the causes and treatments of these disorders, and exciting new research has taught us a great deal in the past few decades.

The fact that many new and successful treatments are available makes it especially important that we reject old prejudices and outmoded ideas that consider mental disorders to be untreatable. If psychological problems are identified early, it is possible to prevent serious conse-quences. We should not keep these problems hidden or feel shame that we or a member of our family has a mental disorder. Some people believe that something they said or did caused a mental disorder. Some people think that these disorders are "only in your head" so that you could "snap out of it" if you made the effort. This type of thinking implies that a treatment is a matter of willpower or motivation. It is a terrible burden for someone who is suffering to be blamed for his or her misery, and often people with psychological disorders are not treated compassionately. We hope that the information in this book will teach you about various mental illnesses.

The problems covered in the volumes of the ENCYCLOPEDIA OF PSYCHOLOGICAL DISORDERS were selected because they are of particular importance to young adults, because they affect them directly, or because they affect family and friends. There are individual volumes on reading disorders, attention deficit and disruptive behavior disorders, and dementia—all of these are related to our abilities to learn and integrate information from the world around us. There are books on drug abuse that provide useful information about the effects of these drugs and treatments that are available for those individuals who have drug problems. Some of the books concentrate on one of the most common mental disorders, depression. Others deal with eating disorders, which are dangerous illnesses that affect a large number of young adults, especially women.

Most of the public attention paid to these disorders arises from a particular incident involving a celebrity that awakens us to our own vulnerability to psychological problems. These incidents of celebrities or public figures revealing their own psychological problems can also enable us to think about what we can do to prevent and treat these types of problems.

Hallucinations and delusions are common symptoms of schizophrenia. This fifteenth-century engraving depicts the early monk St. Anthony being tormented by demons. Today's demons may take different forms than those shown here, but they are no less troubling to the sufferer.

OVERVIEW: SCHIZOPHRENIA

Are they blessed or are they crazy? In some early societies, people who saw "visions" and communicated with "voices" were thought of as holy, even as messengers of the gods. In others, they were considered mad. But most people who experience visions or voices actually have a psychological disorder.

The most common such disorder is schizophrenia. In reality, schizophrenics are neither blessed nor "crazy." They are people whose minds are filled with uncontrollable, torturing thoughts and whose lives are filled with fear and loneliness.

For years, in Western society, schizophrenics were banished to asylums, or to the streets, or to locked rooms inside their family homes, where they lived out their days in misery. Sometimes they were said to be possessed by devils. Even today, schizophrenics are often the butt of cruel, insensitive treatment. Comedians sometimes tell jokes about schizophrenia—or about what they *think* is schizophrenia.

In one typical joke, for instance, a man complains that his wife thinks she's a parking meter.

"Schizophrenia," says the psychiatrist at once. "I can help her, but it'll cost a lot of money."

"No problem. She probably has several hundred dollars in dimes and quarters crammed in her mouth right now."

Schizophrenia, of course, is no laughing matter. Fortunately, modern psychological professionals have learned much about the disease: how to distinguish it from other mental disorders, how to treat it, how to care for its sufferers and help them lead normal lives in society. Most important, perhaps, they have done much to make people aware that there is nothing evil—or funny—about this condition. But schizophrenia, like many other kinds of psychological disorders, remains largely a mystery.

Experts estimate that 1 in every 100 individuals suffers from schizophrenia. Gender and race seem to make little difference in the likelihood that any given individual will develop the illness. It usually strikes during the teen years or early adulthood and most often lasts a lifetime. Investigators have found no one cause or group of causes for the disorder. And though it can be treated successfully, no permanent cure has so far been discovered.

What is life like for a schizophrenic? It's a horrible confusion in which imaginings and reality become so intertwined that the person cannot distinguish between them. Schizophrenics clearly hear what no one around them hears, clearly see what no one else sees, and find it almost impossible to believe that these voices and visions lie in their imagination. Life is a dream—often a terrifying dream that they accept as vicious reality—day and night, with no hope of escape by simply "waking up."

The world, in the minds of many schizophrenics, seems filled with critics, persecutors, even assassins. Others believe themselves to possess fantastic mental and physical powers. They often develop anxiety and abnormal sleeping and eating habits. It's a lonely, despairing, sometimes exhausting existence. Often, the sufferer becomes distant and begins to retreat from society. In severe cases, the schizophrenic may stop interacting altogether.

Ultimately, the person's thoughts may turn to suicide as the only way out. The incidence of attempted suicide is extraordinarily high among schizophrenics, and the actual death rate is chilling.

Doctors' efforts to treat the disorder are complicated by the fact that it appears in many different forms with many different symptoms. Drugs that help some patients have no effect at all on others—or cause complicated side effects and have to be discontinued. And for any given patient a drug that works this month may stop working next month. The person may be subjected to continuing experimentation with different drugs until, with luck, the "right" one is chosen.

Yet researchers who study schizophrenia, like those who are devoted to solving the riddles of other mental and physical disorders, continue to work and to hope. The overall pace of discovery about the functioning of the human body is increasing at a staggering rate. Every week, newspapers and magazines run stories of some startling new discovery about the brain, or genes, or body chemistry. Schizophrenia researchers believe that someday they *will* find a cure and will be able to offer effective preventive measures.

In this volume of the ENCYCLOPEDIA OF PSYCHOLOGICAL DISORDERS we'll look at schizophrenia from the patient's perspective and also from the viewpoint of loved ones, whose own lives are often devastated by the disorder. We'll examine the suspected causes and the warning signals. We'll explore the history of the disease and learn how schizophrenics are being treated today. Finally, we'll see that with proper care and treatment, and with love and assistance from friends and family, many schizophrenics can lead happy, productive lives.

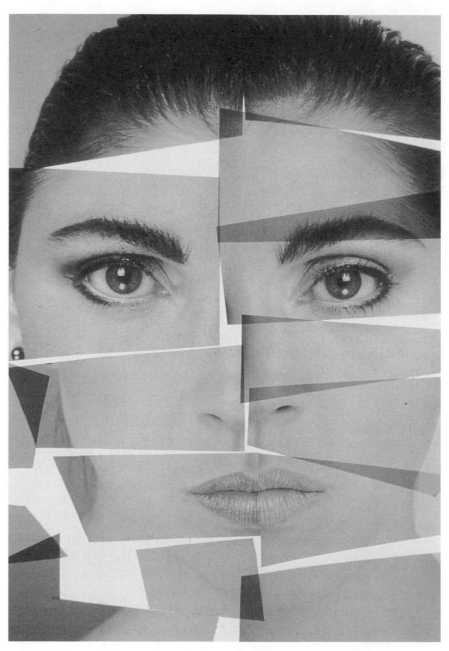

A schizophrenic is likely to feel fragmented, disoriented, or detached from reality. In this artist's rendering, the schizophrenic is made up of pieces that do not fit together properly to make a whole person.

1

WHERE DO I FIND THE REAL WORLD?

Schizophrenia affects a vast number of people. With a frequency rate of 1 person in every 100, it is a relatively common condition. Overall, its cost to society in medical fees and lost income is enormous.

To understand what schizophrenia is like, let's look at several case studies—stories of actual people who have experienced the disorder.

A FRIEND TURNED ENEMY

"The Principal" is a very powerful individual—but no one at Westside High can see or hear him. No one, that is, but Warren, a Westside sophomore. The Principal lives inside Warren's head. He tells Warren what he should do and criticizes him severely when Warren does something wrong.

Oddly, when Warren's mind invented him, The Principal was his closest friend—one of very few friends Warren had. Living in a fantasy world that enveloped his physical world, Warren used to confide in The Principal when he could confide in no one else. The Principal was like a wonderful, wise big brother. He was Warren's friend and no one else's. Warren enjoyed that idea.

In time, though, The Principal became very demanding. Today, he exercises a horrible grip on Warren's whole life. He controls not only how Warren acts but, in many ways, how he thinks. If Warren becomes absorbed in a school activity, a book, a real-life friendship, The Principal soon intrudes. He makes Warren feel guilty for enjoying himself. If Warren does something The Principal doesn't like, this domineering tyrant screams at him. The Principal won't leave Warren to himself. And Warren doesn't know how to make him go away.

To Warren, The Principal is very, very real. Warren figures everyone else has a Principal in their lives, too. Why, he wonders, do other students seem so much happier than he does? They seem to enjoy school projects and books and sports and movies and music and social interaction, all without being

This young schizophrenic is feeling alone and withdrawn. Often sufferers of this mental illness feel so different from the rest of society that they don't even attempt to communicate with peers or family members.

yelled at by their Principals. Yet, for Warren, just being a student and a teenager is a daily struggle. What is going on?

Shannon is one of Warren's classmates. He likes her very much, and she seems to like him. They talk about many things, share ideas, and have good times together. Unlike everyone else, she seems to understand him—or at least she seems willing to accept him. On two or three occasions, he has hinted to her the existence of his great antagonist. But she seems puzzled when he does, so he quickly changes the subject. Maybe, he thinks, other people don't have their own Principals, after all. Warren decides he can never tell Shannon or even his mother about The

Principal. They may think he is insane. A person inside your head, telling you what to do and say? The idea sometimes sounds absurd even to Warren.

This terrible secret has made life miserable for Warren. He's spending far too much time with The Principal, trying to please him. In class, he finds it increasingly hard to concentrate on the material and understand it. He thinks in "fragments." Apart from his friendship with Shannon, he has practically no social life. His parents are alarmed that he will become even more withdrawn as he grows older.

SURROUNDED BY DEMONS

Kelly cannot remember a time when she wasn't having hallucinations and regarding everyone around her with suspicion. In many ways her life has been like that of a drug addict. Yet, Kelly has never misused drugs.

Now approaching 40, she has been undergoing treatment for her psychological disorder since she was a teenager. On numerous occasions, she has had to be admitted to a hospital—sometimes for weeks and months on end.

Like Warren, Kelly has a "Principal" character at work in her mind. But her Principal is just one of many imaginary people with whom she lives. As you might imagine, trying to coexist with them and keep them all happy is extremely difficult. Sometimes, Kelly says, it's as though a telephone operator is laboring inside her head to manage the communications between these imaginary beings. The task is too much for the operator. Messages get crossed up. "Confusion" is hardly the word to describe the resulting mess. "Fragmented thinking" is how people often refer to this condition.

With careful, ongoing treatment, Kelly today is able to manage her illness and her life with some success. But she will never forget the past years of crisis and terror, when people around her sometimes appeared to be demons. She would imagine they had sharp fangs and, like wild beasts, were vying to tear her to pieces. They made her daily life a living nightmare. They were so real to her that often at night, unable to sleep, she would wander around her house, trying to roust them from their hiding places.

Yet, real as these many threatening creatures were to her, Kelly realized something was wrong in her life. She knew her family and acquaintances thought she was "crazy," and part of her could understand why.

Edward Gingerich, an Old Amish man, was found guilty of the 1993 beating death of his wife after he stopped taking medication for schizophrenia. With medication many schizophrenics can lead normal lives, but some may be fooled into thinking that they will feel just as good without their medication.

She, too, feared going insane. What was happening to her? And why her? These were torturous questions.

Kelly remembers the endless tests doctors conducted when she agreed to seek help, while in college. She wasn't at all confident they understood her problems and needs. But she agreed to try the medicine they prescribed. Thorazine, a common medication for certain symptoms of psychological disorders, was the first of almost a dozen prescriptions she tried. Most of the drugs helped her, but only temporarily. Her false beliefs would eventually return.

And most of the medicines brought with them unpleasant side

effects. In fact, Kelly often thought of the drugs as poisons, and she would secretly stop using them. Soon afterward, her mind again would be filled with a Pandora's box of imaginary characters. Usually, Kelly would have to be hospitalized and given new medication.

On two occasions, Kelly attempted suicide. Strangely, her objective wasn't to escape her hellish world, but to punish herself. Kelly felt guilty for letting herself be so sick.

Today, Kelly's life is relatively stable. Having earned a master's degree, she holds down a full-time professional job. For many years she has been treated by a psychiatrist and a therapist, both of whom she fully trusts. They work closely with her and let her know they care about her health. When a medication seems to stop working, they manage to find an effective replacement. They constantly look for the right medications and the correct dosages that will help Kelly fight her mental illness while leaving her with a minimum of unpleasant side effects. Kelly credits them with literally saving her life.

Even though careful medication and therapy—combined with loving support from her family—help Kelly lead a normal life, she knows she is dependent. She has not been cured, but she is far better.

A TEENAGER'S SINISTER CHANGES

Morgan, like Kelly, has battled mental illness for many years as she enters middle age. Although she, too, has been blessed with successful treatment and care, Morgan is often depressed. She wonders what her life would be like today, what she might have accomplished already, had she not been stricken with this disease.

Her doctors suspect Morgan's problem may have a hereditary component; one of her aunts was known to have suffered mental illness. But it wasn't until she was in her late teens that Morgan's personality began to change significantly—and darkly. A once sociable young girl, she became introverted and moody. She felt friendless. Everyone she knew seemed to annoy her. She increasingly felt cut off from everyone else on the planet.

As the symptoms were worsening, Morgan found herself leaving home to begin college. It was a frightening time. She was not happy living with her family, who regarded her with a mixture of love and confusion—but she was terrified at the prospect of "leaving the nest." Arriving at the university, rather than forge much-needed new friendships, she withdrew from all social interaction.

Her abnormal behavior became apparent even to casual observers. Not only was she basically friendless; she refused to speak to anyone. In class, she ignored the lectures and spent her time scribbling poems and sketches in her notebooks. Her physical health weakened drastically, for it rarely occurred to her to eat a regular meal. She would go to bed fully dressed. Some days she would forget to bathe herself.

It was only a matter of time until these physical symptoms culminated in a psychological episode. Morgan began hearing strange voices. To her, the imaginary speakers became as real as the bustling university life around her.

Morgan's family had her admitted to a hospital. Her mother later told friends how shocked she was to discover that her daughter—once bright, attractive and likable—had become so sick.

After exhaustive testing, psychiatrists placed her on medication that relieved her psychotic symptoms. (The term "psychotic" usually implies some disconnection from reality or inability to function on a daily basis.) But Morgan never took the treatment seriously, and she never fully trusted her doctors or their findings. For the next decade, she was in and out of psychiatric hospitals. She calls those her "lost years."

Finally, in her late 20s, Morgan vowed to take control of her life. She wasn't able to conquer her mental illness completely, but by following doctors' prescriptions and advice, she managed to avoid hospitalization.

Then, sadly, she stopped taking her medication. Symptoms of her illness returned, this time more seriously. For a while, she tried to deny the problem. But she couldn't. The maddening voices haunted her day and night.

Happily, Morgan has found an excellent "halfway house" for persons with psychological disorders. As a resident there, she now has a comfortable base from which to receive treatment and to participate in the world around her. With the help of the staff and of her doctors, she is putting the pieces of her life back together.

It is no easy process. She is regaining her confidence, but there are relapses into her old world. "I've come to expect bad times along with the good times," she says. "I try to focus on the good times."

A LIFETIME OF TROUBLE

Dale is 49 years old, and he's been in and out of hospitals for the past 32 years. He suffers from recurring delusions—false beliefs about himself and the outside world.

These young teens are participating in a group counseling session. Adolescence is a difficult time for all young people, but it can be particularly frightening for schizophrenics.

Dale has not been gainfully employed since he was fired from his job as a store clerk in 1982. He has lived with relatives and friends, in halfway houses for the mentally disturbed, and—for several brief periods—on the street. Six years ago, Dale's aging mother made a bold decision: She resolved to bring him home to live with her. His mother died soon afterward, but his younger sister Melanie, who inherited the family home, accepted him into her care.

Melanie was only 10 when her older brother's bizarre behavior started. She remembers her childhood discomfort at his strange moods, but she was shielded from the circumstances of his traumatic early manhood. At any rate, she could not have understood what was going on—and she had too many adolescent interests of her own to pay much attention to Dale's worsening drama. He was just "different." This much she knew, and it was all she wanted to know. After all, if she thought too much about it, she might become "different" like him.

After she graduated from high school and went away to college,

Melanie occasionally spoke to her brother by phone, but she rarely saw him. "Dale" and "family tension" meant the same thing to her. Her brother was someone to be avoided. When she graduated from college, Melanie moved all the way across the country to take a job—not because it was the best offer she had, but because it would remove her from the problem of her brother.

The good news for Dale is that Melanie, in her heart of hearts, never lost her love for her troubled brother. As she matured, she realized how much he would need her when their parents were gone. At their mother's death, she returned to live in the family home and to do what she could to improve her brother's life. It has not been an easy responsibility.

TWO SISTERS

Min and Stacey are sisters in their early 20s. Both have tragic health problems, but of a very different nature.

Min suffers from multiple sclerosis, a disease of the central nervous system that results in loss of coordination and weakened muscles. Her

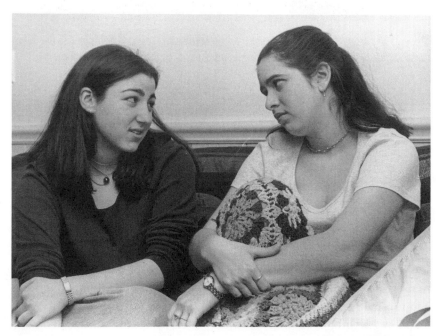

Schizophrenia, like many other mental illnesses, often has few outward signs. Although these two friends appear to have much in common, could one of them be struggling with schizophrenia?

declining health means she needs much special care—and she receives it. Because her disability is "visible," it seems that relatives and friends of the family are constantly going out of their way to help her. They arrange to take her places. They visit. They bring her gifts. They let her know they care. This gives Min some much needed emotional support.

Stacey, on the other hand, has schizophrenia. Her illness is not so "visible," although it has led to similar results, such as an inability to hold a job or interact naturally in social settings. Relatives and family acquaintances—she has few real "friends"—don't often visit Stacey, bring her things, or take her places. Rather, they avoid her. They believe she is simply weird and lazy. They think she has made a calculated decision to be different, to refuse to live up to her potential. They suspect she uses her troubled state of mind to get away with behavior that's unacceptable in "normal" young adults. Often, they phone the women's parents to ask how Min is doing, but they never mention Stacey. They wish she did not exist. And Stacey senses this.

■ ■ ■

Warren, Kelly, Morgan, Dale, and Stacey have all been diagnosed as suffering from schizophrenia. Their stories can be found on the website of the British Columbia Schizophrenia Society and in Janice Jordan's article "Schizophrenia—Adrift in an Anchorless Reality." (See the Bibliography and Further Reading sections at the end of the book for these and other sources.)

The symptoms of schizophrenia usually begin while the person is a teenager or young adult. Thankfully, they can be treated, but most patients learn they must expect a lifelong battle with the disease.

Because of the confusion and the ultimate sense of hopelessness brought on by this illness, it is estimated that as many as half of its victims attempt suicide at some point during their struggle. Which brings us to the most tragic news about schizophrenia: about 1 in 10 of these suicide attempts will succeed.

Although the term schizophrenia literally refers to a "split" mind, the disease is very different from multiple personality disorder. Schizophrenia is actually a complex collection of symptoms.

UNDERSTANDING SCHIZOPHRENIA

"Split personality." For many years that's how people described the effects of schizophrenia. "There are really two (or more!) people living inside one body," they said. Often one of the personalities was thought of as "good," the other "bad." They seemed like the good Dr. Henry Jekyll and the evil "Edward Hyde" in Robert Louis Stevenson's classic novel.

Interestingly, the *Diagnostic and Statistical Manual of Mental Disorders, Fourth Edition (DSM-IV)*, which contains a long discussion of schizophrenia and other psychotic disorders, never uses the term "split personality." The *DSM-IV* is the standard reference on psychological disorders.

Why would the psychological profession's main resource avoid the idea of a "split personality"? Undoubtedly, it's because that term is far too simplistic to describe a disorder that's anything but simple. In some ways, the phrase is even misleading. Schizophrenia is so complex, in fact, that no detailed definition of it seems to apply clearly to every person who suffers from the disorder.

Though commonly referred to as a disease, schizophrenia might better be thought of as what doctors call a syndrome. A disease is usually a fully described illness with a known cause, pattern of progress, or both. A syndrome is a collection of symptoms that are likely to show up together but that do not have a single, easily identifiable cause. Persons who suffer from schizophrenia provide descriptions of their symptoms that have much in common. And they do not paint a pretty picture.

SCHIZOPHRENIA: THE BASICS

Schizophrenia apparently knows no bounds in selecting its victims, and it is not preventable. It seems to affect men and women equally. It has been observed in every major country, culture, social class, and race on earth. It attacks people across a broad range of intelligence, interests, and lifestyles.

Its symptoms are usually noticed first, as mentioned earlier, between the ages of 16 and 30. On the British Columbia website, schizophrenia is called "youth's greatest disabler." Male victims tend to show their first signs while in their early 20s, female victims while in their 20s. The illness can begin later in life, but it is unusual to see preliminary symptoms after age 40. Though also uncommon in preteens, it has been diagnosed in children as young as five.

WHAT, EXACTLY, IS THE PROBLEM?

We'll explore in detail the medical definition of schizophrenia in the next chapter. In simple terms, we might think of it as a mental condition that makes it hard for an individual to distinguish between reality and imagination. This condition may be constant, or it may occur only some of the time. Some people describe schizophrenia as dreaming while you are awake. "But we all daydream," you may say. "We all like to imagine how things should be, as opposed to how things actually are. We all seek to escape reality from time to time. After all, when we read a novel or watch a movie or a TV sitcom, aren't we turning off reality and turning on our imaginations?"

This schizophrenic is tormented by a fantasy world she cannot escape. Often the struggle to deal with their illness leaves schizophrenics exhausted and without hope.

The life of a schizophrenic is very, very different—and terrifying. The mentally well person enjoys an entertaining escape by choice, then decides when it's time to return to reality. (Simply close the book. Turn off the television.) The schizophrenic has no such control. There are few "anchors to reality." Fantasy and real life constantly merge, and the sufferer cannot separate the two. In Jordan's article, schizophrenia is likened to traveling through "a world of madness no one can understand—particularly the person traveling through it."

In order to cope, the schizophrenic usually tries to withdraw from reality. One result: utter loneliness. Meanwhile, the fantasy world into which the person tries to escape may be anything but pleasant. More likely, it is a torment. As the victim struggles to determine what in life is real, he or she becomes confused and exhausted. Thoughts fragment. The person feels physically fatigued.

One patient, quoted in E. Fuller Torrey's *Surviving Schizophrenia*, explained that she would see herself as from a distance, like "watching another girl wear your clothes and carrying out actions as you think them." A noted actress said a large part of her fight to cope with schizophrenia was a matter of waiting—"waiting for the brain to reconnect," according to the British Columbia Schizophrenia Society.

The schizophrenic person is constantly confused and anxious, though withdrawn and often quiet. The person may ignore her or his surroundings and sit completely still and silent for hours. At other times, she or he may be in a frenzy of activity while most other people are sleeping. And there are times in between when the person just seems "blank," speaking in a monotone and displaying neither joy nor sadness nor any other emotion.

When they are talking, the person's thought process may become fragmented. Distracted, the speaker may be unable to finish expressing a simple idea. Or he or she may be unable to connect logical causes and reactions. Hearing of a tragedy or crisis might make the person laugh unexplainably; telling a joke might produce sadness.

HAS IT ALWAYS BEEN A PROBLEM?

Schizophrenia is not a "modern" disease, although it was not given its name until the 20th century. It is believed to have affected people throughout history, in virtually every society. The response to the illness at different times and in different cultures has varied widely.

In many tribal societies, both ancient and modern, those who have "visions" were thought to be blessed or visited by the gods. Some of these people were certainly inspired; others appear to have been schizophrenic or otherwise disturbed. Often they were given a place in society outside the normal structure and referred to as shamans—"medicine men"—with special powers. When Christianity became the major religion of the Western world, it turned the shamans of pagan times into witches. The common people still went to them for advice and treatment, but the church taught that witches were evil and, during the Middle Ages, burned them at the stake.

Later, as the pagan religions died out in western Europe, people who exhibited bizarre mental behavior were thought to be possessed by devils. Consequently, doctors rarely tried to treat them with medication. The mentally disturbed were usually either locked in a lonely room by their families or, if the family could not provide for them or refused to live with the embarrassment of an "insane" relative, cast into the streets. If they committed a crime—or even if they were unjustly accused—they were imprisoned and often kept permanently in chains.

Finally, during the 1800s, Western society began to regard the mentally ill more humanely. Early experiments to treat them and provide therapy gradually grew into an active field of specialized medical research. Doctors increasingly began to realize that "insanity" actually included a broad range of different kinds of disorders with different symptoms. As the 20th century progressed, researchers learned that different kinds of treatment were called for, depending on the specific type of mental illness. Some mental disorders seemed more easily treatable than others.

The word "schizophrenia" was used by the Swiss psychiatrist Eugen Bleuler in 1911 to describe the condition of a group of patients, though many years passed before the term was clearly defined. Earlier, in the 19th century, the disorder was known as *dementia praecox*.

HALLUCINATIONS AND DELUSIONS

Inside their fantasy world, schizophrenics are plagued by hallucinations and delusions. You have probably heard those terms before, perhaps in connection with drug abuse. Some people mistakenly assume they mean the same thing, but they are different.

A hallucination is a false perception. The person imagines something to be real, when it is not. The hallucination may be something the person sees, hears, or even smells. It involves a particular experience—an imagined experience—grounded in one of the senses. The individual may hear a voice no one else hears. Or he may smell smoke and panic at the fear of a house fire, when in reality nothing is burning.

A delusion is a false belief. Such a thought pattern may continue for a long time. In schizophrenia, for example, the person may be under the delusion that he or she is able to perform some impossible feat of strength or talent. The schizophrenic may believe himself or herself to be a famous author, actor, or past or present head of state. The individual may become absorbed in a particular television serial and believe that one of the stars is a personal friend or that the TV show is actually the scenario of the viewer's real life.

On the darker side is the delusion of being persecuted or conspired against, commonly referred to as *paranoia*. Schizophrenics may be under the delusion of being followed everywhere, constantly watched, or blamed for everything that goes wrong. They may suspect that others are cheating them, making fun of them, spreading unkind rumors about them, or poisoning them.

THE HIGH RATE OF SUICIDE

"Weird," you say. "But what's the big deal? Almost everyone occasionally has feelings of overconfidence or, at the opposite end of the emotional spectrum, insecurity. Can't schizophrenics just learn to 'deal with it'?"

The illness is much more serious than most "normal" people can envision. It's so overwhelming and so much a part of mental life that the person can't just "deal with it." This state of mind causes unrelenting anguish over time. Sufferers sometimes burst out angrily. Many consider the ultimate escape: suicide. Several sources confirm that a woefully high percentage of schizophrenics—an estimated 40 to 50 percent—actually attempt it.

Ironically, suicide attempts are *not* usually triggered by the victim's imaginary voices or various delusions. Instead, they occur most frequently during cycles when the disorder has eased somewhat in a person's life. When the individual is able to think more clearly and to understand the depth of the problem, he or she is likely to feel depressed and hopeless. In other words, people who are keenly aware of their sickness are more likely to resort to suicide than are those who deny there is anything wrong with them.

Similarly, some have suggested that schizophrenics are most at risk

The body of this suicide victim was found in New York's Central Park Reservoir. Most schizophrenics face a lifetime of struggle with their illness, and many attempt suicide, often more than once. About 10 percent of people with schizophrenia succeed in taking their own lives.

during times of the year that are especially happy for most people. In springtime, for instance, people in cool climates see an end to cabin fever and look forward to warm days. Flowers are blossoming everywhere, signaling renewed life. The schizophrenic, by contrast, sees no hope of finding a fresh start in her or his personal life. It can be a particularly depressing season. Birthdays and holidays such as Christmas are also very trying.

Some of the most common reasons depressed people consider suicide are deep personal loss (death of a close relative or friend, breakup of a long-standing romantic relationship, termination of a job) and a sense of worthlessness. Schizophrenia often contributes to the loss of friendships and employment. So among people with psychological disorders, schizophrenics are at high risk of attempting suicide.

Suicide is most likely to prey on an individual's mind when he or she

ART AND SCHIZOPHRENIA

Artists of all kinds—painters, sculptors, musicians, storytellers, writers—have always held a special place in society. At the same time, people have found the personalities of many artists to be strange. Michelangelo and Vincent van Gogh, for example, were difficult people whose behavior could be unsettling. The 20th century, in particular, witnessed several highly publicized suicides among musicians and writers.

Studies conducted during the last two decades have shown that certain mental aberrations are sometimes associated with intense forms of artistic creativity. This certainly does not mean that all artists are "crazy" or that all people who are psychologically ill can become artists. Rather, it seems to indicate that certain types of mental activity may be shared by artistic personalities and people with mental disorders. Recently, the National Alliance for Research on Schizophrenia and Depression (NARSAD) put together a traveling show of artwork created by people with various psychological disorders.

Vincent van Gogh suffered from mental illness in his later years and committed suicide when he despaired of recovering. The relationship between artistic ability and mental illness has fascinated researchers for decades.

The Russian ballet dancer and choreographer Vaslav Nijinsky, considered one of the greatest male dancers of all time, succumbed to schizophrenia at the height of his career and dropped out of public life.

Though there is usually no way to identify who, in the past, suffered from schizophrenia, it is likely that certain artists were schizophrenic. Van Gogh, for example, a celebrated 19th-century Dutch painter, was institutionalized twice and died of a self-inflicted gunshot wound.

Vaslav Nijinsky, considered the greatest male ballet dancer of the 20th century, toured Europe and the Americas before World War I to the same sort of acclaim as today's rock stars. But his career lasted only 12 years. Diagnosed with schizophrenia in 1919, he lived until 1950 but never danced on stage again. It has also been suggested that the Austrian writer Franz Kafka, whose short stories and novels written early in the 20th century have influenced artists of all types, was schizophrenic. Many of his works are filled with feelings of paranoia.

Other artists, less familiar now but well known in their day, were diagnosed with *dementia praecox*, or schizophrenia, as it was later called. English painter Richard Dadd (1819–1886) developed schizophrenia and murdered his father. Helped by understanding doctors, he recovered some of his health and continued to paint, but in a more hallucinatory way. Early in the 20th century, the European artist Louis Wain painted pictures of almost nothing but cats. After he developed schizophrenia, the faces of his cats took on a hostile, sinister cast, and the bodies were fragmented.

The paintings of the Russian artist Gemady Ustyugov were suppressed by the Soviet government in the 1960s. Since the fall of the Soviet Union, his art has been shown in major exhibits. Ustyugov was diagnosed with schizophrenia early in his artistic career, and his paintings, though not violent, have a sad, uncomfortable feeling. He has said that "thoughts arrive, thoughts leave, and my soul does not find anything here."

One of the most wrenching portrayals of schizophrenia is the song "Mr. Whisper," written and performed by the singer Dory Previn on her first album, *On My Way to Where* (1970). Previn, who had an intense fear of flying, was removed, screaming, from a plane, institutionalized, and treated with electroconvulsive therapy. She describes her experience and thoughts in strong, painful detail.

Similarly, and perhaps even more powerfully, an author using the pseudonym Barbara O'Brien wrote a book called *Operators and Things* (now, unfortunately, out of print). A tremendously talented writer, she brought to life the delusions, hallucinations, turmoil, and fear experienced by the schizophrenic as few other artists have ever managed to do.

is alone for extended periods. Caregivers of schizophrenics know the importance of frequent communication. If the ill person lives away from home, caregivers visit, telephone, and write postcards or letters often.

A MYSTERIOUS—AND MISUNDERSTOOD—DISORDER

Most people do not fully understand the nature of schizophrenia. (Perhaps only a person who has lived through the disease can really know what it's like.) Therefore, they often regard it with fear and aren't particularly eager to spend time with individuals known to suffer from schizophrenia.

Public suspicion results partly from the reputation the disorder has acquired. Television shows, movies, and novels sometimes identify violent and tragic characters as schizophrenics. From time to time, when sensational criminals are caught and psychologically evaluated, they are reported to suffer from schizophrenia or some other mental disorder. In the public's mind, the disease thus becomes identified with the violent acts of a particular villain.

But many doctors and researchers believe schizophrenia is getting a bum rap as an allegedly "violent" disease. Some studies suggest that persons with psychological disorders, including this one, are no more prone to violence than the general population.

Actually, as discussed above, schizophrenics seem far more inclined to withdraw into their private worlds than to commit public acts of violence. They just want to be left alone and are more likely to be timid. And once they enter a treatment program, any tendency toward violence is lessened by the administration of antipsychotic drugs and other medications.

Can schizophrenia be cured? The short answer is that schizophrenia cannot yet be cured, but it can be treated. By strictly following a prescribed plan of care, the victim can lead a productive and relatively happy life.

In view of the large number of persons suffering from schizophrenia, it's quite possible you know schizophrenics but don't realize they have the disease. As long as they are able to control the symptoms with reasonable success, those around them may never be aware of their struggle.

AN UNHAPPY EXISTENCE

Some mental disorders are like roller-coaster rides. A person may suffer disastrous episodes of depression and/or anxiety, for example, and then return to a period of mental "normality" for weeks, months, or even years. But a schizophrenic may not be able to look forward to such long periods of relative peace. In typical cases of schizophrenia, the problems are ongoing, and medication must be taken for the long term.

The disease can have a negative impact on every aspect of a victim's life. For instance:

- School work, specific tasks, or on the job duties may be unusually difficult because the person is unable to concentrate and to make fast, well-thought-out decisions.

- Ordinary conversation, expressing one's feelings, and other social interaction can be so difficult that schizophrenics are often friendless.

- The person may become so preoccupied with the fantasy world that he or she neglects the simplest human functions:

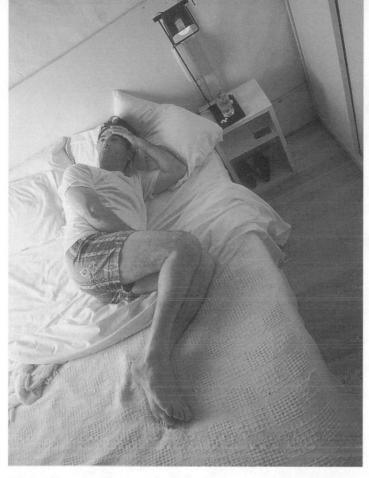

The inability to function normally day to day is common among schizo-phrenics. Like the young man staring off into space here, many people who suffer from this illness withdraw socially and experience an emotional flatness.

healthy meals, tooth brushing and other basic personal hygiene, or regular periods of sleep.

None of this means that schizophrenics always behave strangely. They may follow the patterns of people around them, eating and sleeping at regular times. Most often, they may appear "normal" to a casual observer. And with the proper treatment, they can lead productive lives at work and in school.

There is one positive finding. Unlike such psychological disorders as Alzheimer's disease, schizophrenia apparently does not grow progressively worse with age. Even late in life, most victims can hope for successful treatment.

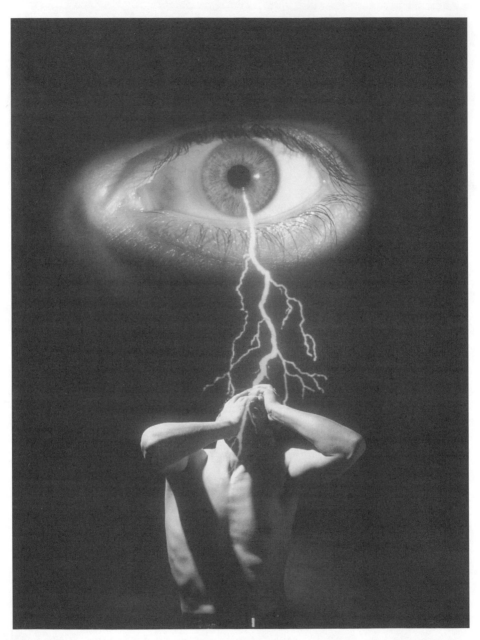

Many schizophrenics suffer from paranoia, the feeling that they are constantly being watched or tormented by others. Paranoia can present special problems to children in school or adults in a work setting.

3

DIAGNOSIS

How does the *Diagnostic and Statistical Manual of Mental Disorders, Fourth Edition (DSM-IV)* characterize schizophrenia? As we've already seen, it is not easy to describe. Schizophrenia is one type of "psychotic" disorder—but the meaning of the word "psychotic" has changed over the years.

Narrowly defined, a psychosis is a mental abnormality involving delusions or "prominent hallucinations." (We discussed the difference between delusions and hallucinations in Chapter 2.) But some researchers prefer a broader definition. To them, the term "psychosis" can also include fractured speech, a frustrating inability to organize and plan things, and even catatonic action—a radical stiffening or loosening of the limbs and muscles as part of an unnatural mental response to experiences. Others have used a still looser definition of psychosis, citing any "impairment that grossly interferes with the capacity to meet ordinary demands of life."

The *DSM-IV* includes schizophrenia under the label of psychotic disorders, but it takes a middle road in defining "psychotic." When applied to schizophrenia and related disorders, the term "psychotic," it states, "refers to delusions, any prominent hallucinations, disorganized speech, or disorganized or catatonic behavior."

In this context, the *DSM-IV* describes schizophrenia as "a disturbance that lasts for at least six months and includes at least one month of active-phase symptoms (i.e., two [or more] of the following: delusions, hallucinations, disorganized speech, grossly disorganized or catatonic behavior, negative symptoms)." Five subtypes of schizophrenia are defined: paranoid, disorganized, catatonic, undifferentiated, and residual. We will look at these subtypes in some detail later in this chapter.

There are no chemical or genetic tests to prove that a person has schizophrenia. As the *DSM-IV* puts it, "no laboratory findings have been identified

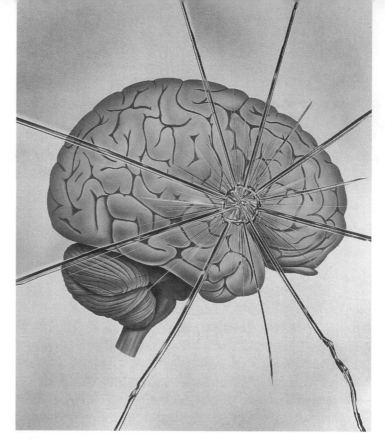

Researchers have found specific structural abnormalities in the brains of people with schizophrenia. This is one artist's interpretation of the brain as resembling a broken piece of glass.

that are diagnostic of schizophrenia. However, a variety of laboratory findings have been noted to be abnormal in groups of individuals with schizophrenia relative to control subjects. Structural abnormalities in the brain have consistently been demonstrated in individuals with schizophrenia as a group." We'll examine some of the research findings later in this book.

Although psychologists can confidently diagnose schizophrenia in most cases, the *DSM-IV* acknowledges that "clinicians may have a tendency to overdiagnose schizophrenia" among certain ethnic groups, because people in different cultures have different ways of expressing themselves verbally and physically.

A CLOSER LOOK AT SCHIZOPHRENIA

Some symptoms of schizophrenia last for a relatively short period (as little as a month). Others persist for six months at a time, or longer.

While suffering from these symptoms, the person finds it difficult to function socially or to perform well in school or on the job.

The symptoms of some other disorders are very similar to those of schizophrenia. Before diagnosing a patient as schizophrenic, doctors must be sure the disturbance isn't better accounted for by one of them. (See "Similar but Different Ailments," in this chapter).

The "dysfunctions" caused by schizophrenia can be of many different types. There can be problems with concentration and reasoning. There can be emotional upsets. There can be halting or nonsensical speech. An apparent attitude of carelessness or a lack of attention may be present. Evidence of one of these dysfunctions alone does not suggest schizophrenia. Rather, schizophrenia encompasses a "constellation" of these symptoms, with resulting social problems or difficulties with school or job performance.

In schizophrenia, these problems in functioning occur in two categories of symptoms: positive and negative. The word "positive" here is not used in a complimentary way. Rather, it designates perhaps the more alarming of the two types of schizophrenic symptoms. It refers to *increased activity*—excessive or distorted thought processes and actions. Positive symptoms, the *DSM-IV* explains, include delusions, hallucinations, confused speech, and grossly disorganized or catatonic behavior. Delusions and hallucinations fall within what psychologists call the "psychotic dimension" of schizophrenia. The other positive symptoms are in what's known as the "disorganization dimension."

"Negative" symptoms, on the other hand, indicate *decreased activity*, a loss of normal functioning ability. The person seems to be listless and unemotional and is unable to express himself or herself (a condition called speech alogia).

Let's examine these two categories of symptoms a little more closely.

POSITIVE SYMPTOMS

We have talked briefly about delusions and hallucinations. Delusions, as we saw, are false beliefs. Usually, they occur when the person misinterprets what's happening in his or her immediate world. Feelings of persecution at one extreme or superiority at the other are two kinds of delusions.

In schizophrenia, persecution is the most common delusion. When a schizophrenic student notices a group of classmates huddled in conversation, for example, and then one of them turns to glance at her, the

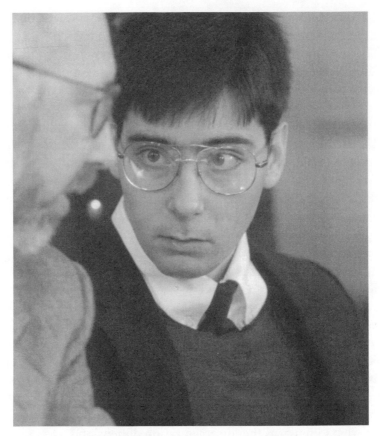

Throughout the trial of John Salvi, charged in connection with the shooting spree at two women's health clinics in Brookline, Massachusetts, his lawyer argued that the defendant was a delusional schizophrenic. The jury found Salvi guilty of premeditated murder, and he was sentenced to two consecutive life terms. Salvi killed himself in prison by placing a plastic bag over his head.

schizophrenic might feel that she is the subject of a conspiracy. (Everyone occasionally feels paranoid. But the schizophrenic constantly finds evidence of such persecution.)

"Grandiosity" is a kind of delusion in which schizophrenics assume some characteristic that makes them very special. As "descendants of Mozart," for instance, they believe they will someday be (or already are) great pianists and composers. Or they might believe they have the power to read other people's minds or control other people's actions by concentrated thought.

Another type of delusion common in schizophrenia is the "referential" delusion. In this case the individual draws personal meaning from a passing reference—perhaps a statement in a newspaper or book, a line or verse of a song or poem. "They wrote that about *me!*" the person sincerely believes.

It isn't easy to gauge the seriousness of delusions. As we noted, most people from time to time have feelings of paranoia—some more often than others. And there can be a gray area between a grandiose delusion and ordinary ego. Some people think they are exceptionally gifted athletes, singers, or writers, when in fact their talents and abilities are at best average.

Cultural traditions can affect a person's behavior in ways that seem, incorrectly, delusional to observers from other cultures. Religious dance rituals, karate training, and even yoga exercise can seem bizarre to someone totally unfamiliar with those practices and their purposes.

Psychologists have to sort out the difference between "delusion," "strongly held belief," and simple tradition in evaluating patients who may be schizophrenic. Special care is called for if the person is from a different culture than that of the examiner.

Hallucinations, unlike delusions, are not ingrained, ongoing beliefs. They are imaginary experiences that involve the senses (sight, hearing, smell, etc.). By far the most frequently occurring hallucinations in schizophrenia are sounds: "voices" often develop in the person's mind. Sometimes the voices are those of familiar people, sometimes not. These experiences are not the schizophrenic hearing himself or herself think; they are encounters with separate beings. Nor are they isolated occurrences (for example, thinking you hear your name called when you're half awake or in noisy surroundings). Such experiences occur regularly.

The voices may be friendly, but they are more frequently critical, even threatening. Sometimes the schizophrenic hears two or more voices talking to one another. Sometimes the voices keep up an endless commentary about what the schizophrenic is thinking or doing.

A less common form of hallucination in schizophrenia is visual. The person may believe there's a window in a wall where no window really exists. Or he or she may "see" a ghost or a wild animal poised to attack.

Beyond delusions and hallucinations lie a number of other positive symptoms that are less frequently encountered. Disorganized thinking, or "formal thought disorder," is hard to define. It is most obvious in the person's speech. The individual may lose the train of conversation, mak-

SIMILAR BUT DIFFERENT AILMENTS

Psychotic symptoms like those associated with schizophrenia are seen in numerous kinds of medical conditions. The *DSM-IV* describes several similar disorders, including these:

- **Schizophreniform disorder:** This is similar to schizophrenia except that it lasts only one to six months and does not necessarily involve a decline in functioning.

- **Schizoaffective disorder:** In this type of disturbance, a mood episode and active schizophrenic symptoms occur together. ("Moods," in medical terms, are just what you probably envision. They range from depression to euphoria.) At least two weeks of delusions or hallucinations, without serious mood symptoms, occur before or after the mood episode.

- **Shared psychotic disorder:** This involves two people. One person develops a psychotic disturbance as a result of the influence of another person who suffers from a similar delusion.

- **Psychotic disorder due to a general medical condition:** A disorder in which the psychotic symptoms result directly from a physical problem.

ing comments and giving answers to questions that are only vaguely related to the subject at hand—or completely unrelated. In some cases, the person's statements are virtually incomprehensible.

"Grossly disorganized behavior," according to the *DSM-IV*, may range from childish silliness to an unkempt or unexplainable appearance. The person might put on several coats on a summer day or wear one dress over another. The individual might be seen urinating in public or suddenly burst out cursing or screaming for no apparent reason.

"Grossly disorganized behavior must be distinguished from behavior that is merely aimless or generally unpurposeful," the *DSM-IV* points out, "and from organized behavior that is motivated by delusional beliefs. Similarly, a few instances of restless, angry, or agitated behavior

• **Substance-induced psychotic disorder:** Drug abuse, poisoning, or strong medication may cause psychotic symptoms much like those seen in schizophrenia.

Other conditions that resemble schizophrenia include forms of dementia (a decline in memory, judgment, and other mental abilities that is especially common among the elderly) and delirium (temporary confusion or display of uncontrolled emotions). These symptoms can also be produced by brain tumors, substance abuse, strong medication, or other medical complications.

As you can see, diagnosing schizophrenia is a difficult, delicate endeavor for psychiatrists. Just because a person experiences delusions or other schizophrenic symptoms, it does not necessarily mean he or she has schizophrenia. The individual may have a far less serious problem—or may have an equally serious psychological disorder, but of a different type.

To pinpoint the exact nature of the patient's illness, examiners must conduct their studies over time and consider not just the recognizable symptoms but related evidence submitted by family members and other observers.

As for the popular misconception that schizophrenics have "split personalities," psychiatrists have indeed identified a disease called "Disossiative Identity Disorder." However, it is very rare and is not a form of schizophrenia. To equate schizophrenia with "split personality" is simply wrong.

should not be considered to be evidence of schizophrenia, especially if the motivation is understandable."

Examples of catatonic symptoms include being oblivious to one's surroundings and sitting rigidly or standing "at attention" for no apparent reason, resisting efforts at being moved. At the other extreme, they can include excessive activity and excitement. Catatonia is seen in other kinds of psychological disorders, such as some mood disorders, and it can also result from the side effects of medication.

NEGATIVE SYMPTOMS

The negative symptoms of schizophrenia include several types of lessening of activity. Although these may seem less obviously alarming than positive symptoms, they too may be a serious indicator of unhealthiness.

"Affective flattening" is a common negative symptom. The schizophrenic may look dazed, not making eye contact or responding to communication. At times the individual may smile and seem to "return to earth," but the expression of any emotions is very limited.

"Alogia" has been defined as "poverty of speech." When questioned, the person will answer, but the responses are short, often meaningless. The individual seems unable to form thoughts into statements. (Of course, she or he may simply not feel like talking. Before it can be characterized as alogia, this symptom must be evident for some time, in varied circumstances.)

"Avolition" is described as "an inability to initiate and persist in goal-directed activities. The person may sit for long periods of time and show little interest in participating in work or social activities." (This, again, must be demonstrated over the long term in a broad context. Compare it, for instance, to common laziness.)

Negative symptoms of schizophrenia are hard to evaluate. Friends, relatives, teachers, employers, and coworkers may be slow to notice them or to suspect their seriousness. And similar behavior can be caused by many different things, some of which have nothing to do with psychological problems (the influences of home life, environment, medication, or substance abuse, for example).

SUBTYPES OF SCHIZOPHRENIA

Psychiatrists have identified five different "subtypes" of the disease.

- **Paranoid type:** "The essential feature . . . is the presence of prominent delusions or auditory hallucinations," according to the *DSM-IV*. In spite of these symptoms, the person's ability to think and communicate with other people seems to be intact. Doctors see few if any signs of disorganized speech or "flat" or catatonic behavior. The delusions, meanwhile, may be many and varied, "but are usually organized around a coherent theme." Anger, anxiety, and a tendency to argue are common characteristics associated with the paranoid type of schizophrenia.

- **Disorganized type:** As the term suggests, this type is characterized by disorganized speech and behavior, along with flat

This schizophrenic is unable to deal with the pile of dirty dishes in her kitchen. People suffering from schizophrenia often feel overwhelmed by ordinary daily tasks.

or inappropriate emotional displays. "The disorganized speech may be accompanied by silliness and laughter that are not closely related to the content of the speech," says the *DSM-IV*. "The behavioral disorganization (i.e., lack of goal orientation) may lead to severe disruption in the ability to perform activities of daily living (e.g., showering, dressing, or preparing meals)." There may be no hallucinations or delusions in this subtype of schizophrenia; if they occur, they are not persistent. The person may exhibit odd facial expressions and physical mannerisms and may have difficulty with thought processes.

- **Catatonic type:** This type is marked by a "psychomotor disturbance." Here "motor" signifies physical movements. Such a disturbance implies unnatural physical motions or positions caused by a psychological influence. Stupor and rigid posture are examples of psychomotor disturbance. The person may have involuntary muscular reactions. There may also be evidence of echolalia ("the pathological, parrotlike, and apparently senseless repetition of a word or phrase just spoken by another person") and echopraxia ("the repetitive imitation of the movements of another person").

- **Undifferentiated type:** Simply put, the symptoms indicate a medical definition of schizophrenia but as a whole they don't fit clearly under any of the three subtypes just discussed.

- **Residual type:** Here the person has suffered at least one definite schizophrenic episode in the past, but at present shows no prominent symptoms. Despite the absence of major hallucinations, delusions, or disorganized behavior, however, clear evidence remains of schizophrenic disturbance. The individual may exhibit a flatness of emotion and expression, or avolition or alogia (defined above). Other symptoms might include strange beliefs or behavior and mild speech impairments.

THE COURSE OF THE DISEASE

The age of most victims at the onset of schizophrenia (when the disorder begins) is early to mid 20s in men, late 20s in women. According to the *DSM-IV*, the onset may be sudden but in most cases is gradual, with early warning signals.

Does the disease affect men and women differently? On average, males tend to exhibit it earlier in life and to suffer more extreme symptoms. In more technical language, the *DSM-IV* explains:

> Individuals with an early age at onset are more often male and have a poorer premorbid [before the disease strikes] adjustment, lower educational achievement, more evidence of structural brain abnormalities, more prominent negative signs and symptoms, more evidence of cognitive impairment as assessed with neuropsychological testing, and a worse outcome. Conversely, individuals with a later onset are more often female, have less evidence of structural brain abnormalities or cognitive impairment, and display a better outcome.

The course of schizophrenia varies. Some victims experience severe episodes followed by remissions (periods without symptoms). Others are constantly sick.

Many young schizophrenic patients feel alone and hopeless. The onset of schizophrenia among young men occurs most often between the ages of 20 and 25.

What are the long-term prospects? "Complete remission (i.e., a return to full premorbid functioning) is probably not common in this disorder," the *DSM-IV* concludes. "Of those who remain ill, some appear to have a relatively stable course, whereas others show a progressive worsening associated with severe disability."

Are some categories of sufferers likely to fare better than others? Perhaps. The *DSM-IV* points to evidence that certain factors seem to be associated with a better prognosis for the disease. "These include good premorbid adjustment, acute onset, later age at onset, being female, precipitating events, associated mood disturbance, brief duration of active-phase symptoms, good interepisode functioning, minimal residual symptoms, absence of structural brain abnormalities, normal neurological functioning, a family history of mood disorder, and no family history of schizophrenia."

Mothers and fathers are sometimes overwhelmed by the task of caring for a schizophrenic child. Caregivers often experience feelings similar to those that occur when someone dies: denial, grief, fear, guilt, and anger.

4

EFFECTS ON CAREGIVERS AND SOCIETY

"Chaotic" is how relatives of someone who is schizophrenic often describe family life under the cloud of their loved one's illness. Parents blame themselves for their child's sickness. Sisters and brothers worry about the social disgrace the illness may bring on the whole family. Caregivers grope desperately for solutions to the ongoing crisis. Too often, the family unit is permanently damaged or destroyed.

According to the British Columbia Schizophrenia Society, families of schizophrenics must learn to deal with issues like these:

- **Denial:** It may be very hard to accept the fact that mental illness has occurred within the family. For a long time, many parents, siblings, and spouses of schizophrenics tell themselves the sick person is just "going through a tough stage in life."

- **Grief:** There is a sense that the loved one has been "lost" forever. The family fear the individual will never again be the person he or she once was and will never become the person they'd hoped to see develop.

- **Fear:** This ranges from minor concern over hurting the person's feelings to agonizing dread that the person will become violent and hurt himself or herself—or someone else. There is also the long-range fear of what will happen to the sick young person later in life, after his or her parents are gone.

- **Guilt:** Parents feel they have done a terrible job of bringing up their child. Sisters, brothers, or spouses feel they have mistreated the person and caused or worsened the illness.

- **Exhaustion**: The strains of caregiving and a feeling of hopelessness leave the family weary. Parents may have difficulty sleeping and

47

This parent may not feel that she can help her schizophrenic daughter, but her very presence may be what the girl needs at a time of crisis.

may lose their appetite; their own health may become frail. In appearance, they may seem to turn gray and "age" rapidly. "We just wish [the sick loved one] would disappear," they sometimes admit after months and years of living with the troubled relative.

- **Anger and bitterness:** "Why is this happening to our family?" relatives ask. They may turn their frustration on "the system" and on the society around them if they live in a city or town where hospital and community support resources are limited. Meanwhile, brothers and sisters of the sick person may grow angry. Siblings may believe the schizophrenic is behaving strangely just to get special attention from the parents, and they may become jealous of the extra attention their brother or sister receives.

- **Loss of control:** Consumed by the crisis, family members may be able to focus on little else in their lives. They may break down crying whenever they try to vent their feelings to close friends. It's not uncommon for family caregivers to seek escape in excessive alcohol use. Schizophrenia becomes for them almost as hellish a nightmare as it is for the patient.

- **Marital problems:** When one spouse is mentally ill, the relationship between husband and wife may become confused and strained. The marriage often deteriorates, leading to divorce.

- **Loss of place in the community:** Because of the stigma attached to the disease (discussed below) and the sheer demands of caregiving, the family may stop participating in community and social functions they once enjoyed.

A TROUBLESOME IMAGE

You've probably heard the word "stigma." Schizophrenia and other mental disorders usually bring with them a stigma, a feeling in the minds of thoughtless observers that the victim's condition reflects disgrace or weakness. Persons with physical disabilities, for example, often feel that a stigma is attached to their bodily disability or their appearance an embarrassed feeling that the world sees them as weak or less than whole. In many cases this stigma lingers for a lifetime, even if the individual learns to cope well with the disability, to live happily, and to contribute important work to society.

To a schizophrenic, who may be inclined to delusions of persecution, overcoming the accompanying stigma is a difficult part of fighting the disease.

Why does society scorn the mentally ill and treat them with suspicion? Fear has much to do with it. People tend to be afraid of things they don't understand. (And, as we have seen, even medical researchers don't fully comprehend schizophrenia.)

When you don't understand something, you can only make assumptions about it. Your own notions about schizophrenia may be based on what you've heard from uninformed friends or even from adults in leadership positions. Very possibly, your opinions are based on characters you've watched in Hollywood productions. Maybe some of your friends have suggested that mental illness is the way certain people are being punished for doing bad things, or that it is caused by something in the person's lifestyle. They may say it's contagious and can be contracted simply by breathing the air close to someone who is mentally ill. All these beliefs are wrong.

Some people fear schizophrenics because they believe they will become violent. As we mentioned earlier, this usually is *not* the case. But if you think certain people or categories of people have criminal intentions by their nature, you're likely to avoid those individuals. And when you hear that they have been hospitalized, you're likely to assume it's because they are dangerous to society—and perhaps always will be.

Couple these unfortunate impressions of the general public with our natural dislike of diseases, and the result is a strongly negative feeling toward schizophrenics and others who suffer from mental disorders. It's easy to understand why people hold misconceptions like these. Society must overcome them, though, if we are to win our battle against psychological disorders. Better education is a key to beating the prejudice and getting on with the fight.

MONEY MATTERS

The most obvious cost of schizophrenia is the cost of treatment. Hospitalization for any disease is increasingly expensive. Medicine is expensive. Therapy sessions are expensive.

The other major cost is measured in lost wages and productivity. While in the throes of severe symptoms, the schizophrenic finds it virtually impossible to hold down a regular job. Bear in mind, too, that lost wages (and entire lost careers) are suffered not only by schizophrenic patients but by many of their caregivers. The drain on everyone involved, in both time and stress, wreaks havoc on normal productivity.

Recent estimates, including some by researchers at the National Institute of Mental Health (NIMH), place the total cost of schizophrenia anywhere between $30 billion and $65 billion annually in the United States alone. These figures combine the direct cost of medical treatment with lost time from work for patients and caregivers and with social and criminal justice services. Of course, it's impossible to calculate a precise figure because of the countless unknowns and variables. But it's clear that, as with other diseases, the price of schizophrenia is escalating each year.

Another monetary issue is the cost of vigorous research to find the cause of the disease as well as improved treatment. Some advocates for

Some schizophrenics develop antisocial behavior, refusing to bathe, change their clothes, and groom themselves. This homeless woman once had a home and family, but her behavior alienated her from those she loved.

improved mental health care believe research in this field has been slow because of slim funding. Most mental disorders do not receive the kind of organized, intense, grant- and government-supported push for cures, backed by a groundswell of public concern, that is given to major physical diseases like cancer, AIDS, and heart defects.

Until fairly recently, mental illness was swept under the rug, kept from public attention. Even now, many people are not aware of the complex needs of schizophrenics and their families—and the costs of meeting those needs. The relative lack of urgency in attacking schizophrenia may also exist because it is not publicized as a leading cause of death or an alarming epidemic. People have less fear of becoming schizophrenic than of contracting one of the primary killer diseases.

The mystery of psychological suffering has intrigued many artists, as in this work by Egon Schiele from the early 20th century. Recently, however, researchers have begun to unravel the mystery by examining possible biological causes.

5

WHAT CAUSES SCHIZOPHRENIA?

Many psychological disorders remain mysteries even after years of research. Why, ultimately, do they arise? Why do they strike some people but not others? Is there anything we can do to prevent them? For schizophrenia in particular, investigators cannot yet give us absolute answers, but they are finding valuable clues.

Researchers constantly consider the role a person's surroundings might play in either causing psychological disorders or triggering the symptoms. At one time, for example, some psychiatrists and mental health workers suspected that schizophrenia resulted solely from bad parenting. Today we know that an unhappy home life does not *cause* schizophrenia, although stress from this kind of unhappiness can make things worse for a schizophrenic.

Recent research on the origins of schizophrenia has focused on physical causes. The possibilities considered have ranged from birth or growth defects to viral infections. The majority of current theories, however, relate in some way to genetic factors, brain chemistry, or both. Let's look at some of these theories.

GENETICS AND FAMILY HISTORIES

Genetics is the biological study of heredity. That is, what physical, mental, or chemical features might have been passed along to you through the genes of your parents? The investigation of genetics began about a century ago, among breeders of plants. Scientists now know that most human characteristics are partly determined (or at least influenced) by a combination of genetic factors.

Schizophrenia seems to run in certain families. Does this automatically mean the disease is inherited? Not necessarily. Suppose, for example, a mother and her son are both diagnosed as schizophrenic. While the genetic factor may be strongly suspected, the situation also might be only a coincidence. What if it is someday proven, as most researchers believe, that a person's environment

The schizophrenic often feels trapped in a bewildering maze. Confusion, inability to concentrate, and loss of memory are common symptoms.

also contributes to the development of psychological disorders? If this is the case, and if the mother and son grow up and live in the same basic surroundings, then their disease might be blamed on either genetics or environment—or on both.

Many investigations, though, have shown probable genetic links. One study noted by the National Alliance for Research on Schizophrenia and Depression (NARSAD) found that schizophrenics with a family history of the disease tended to have more serious childhood behavioral problems than schizophrenics with no such family history. These early child-hood problems may strengthen the case for genetic influences.

The *DSM-IV* states that "first-degree biological relatives [immediate family] of individuals with schizophrenia have a risk for schizophrenia that is about 10 times greater than that of the general population." Studies that compare adopted children of schizophrenic parents with biological children of schizophrenic parents show that the biological children "have a substantially increased risk for schizophrenia." But the *DSM-IV* also points to findings that indicate "the importance of envi-ronmental factors" in determining why certain individuals seem to be affected more than others.

A SCHIZOPHRENIA GENE?

Scientists have looked for a "schizophrenia gene" that might be passed from parent to child. If such a gene can be found, it would point to heredity as a *cause* of the disease, not simply a basis for a schizo-phrenic disposition. But no such gene has been identified.

Though no single gene has been shown to be responsible for schizo-phrenia, scientists are beginning to see that abnormal genes are some-times found more often in schizophrenics than in the general popula-tion. Research conducted with families in which several members have schizophrenia suggests that those members with the disorder are more likely than nonsufferers in the same family to show a particular sequence of genes. This same group of genes has already been linked to another disorder, manic depression (bipolar disorder).

Some studies indicate that schizophrenia may share strange patterns, inside certain genes, with other kinds of brain disorders. One study, reported in *Science News*, found that nucleic acids, the chemical build-ing blocks of genes, sometimes repeat in "nonsense" sequences similar to those seen in a disorder called Huntington's disease. Other research indicates that an abnormal gene may fuel the delusions and other psy-chotic symptoms suffered by schizophrenics.

RISK FACTORS AND FAMILY DECISION MAKING

As we said earlier, schizophrenia is believed to strike approximately 1 person in 100, or 1 percent of the population. One source estimates that if you have a grandparent, aunt, or uncle who is schizophrenic, your

EXPLORING CHANGES
IN THE BRAIN

Until recently, research into brain structure depended almost entirely on cutting open brains during autopsies. This approach could identify major abnormalities but provided no information about how the living brain works.

New imaging techniques, however, have made it possible to study and measure the brain in action without having to operate on it. Most of these techniques have been available for 25 years or less, so the study of living brain structure is a new area of medical science, though one that is expanding rapidly. The research tools include:

- **EEG (electroencephalogram)**, an older technique that records brain waves to see how the brain responds to different types of stimulation
- **CAT (computed axial tomography)**, a computerized imaging technique that uses X rays to provide visual, detailed images of a living person's brain
- **PET (positron-emission tomography)**, which creates images using mild radioactive materials to measure how much energy different parts of the brain are using while processing thoughts or performing other functions
- **MRI (magnetic resonance imaging)**, which uses radio waves and computer analysis of atomic nuclei to obtain precise measurements of brain structures
- **RCBF (regional cerebral blood flow)**, a technique in which the patient inhales a gas that can be observed as it disappears from different regions of the brain, providing information about the brain's activities during thought processes

Though no single change in brain structure separates schizophrenia from any other disorder, several studies of the brain over the last few years (reported in *Science News*) have identified conditions that often seem to go along with being schizophrenic. For example, many experts have long believed that the relatively rare childhood schizophrenia and the more usual form, which starts during late adolescence, might be two different disorders. However, researchers at NIMH have found that children who develop schizophrenia early in life may share brain abnormalities with persons who develop it in their late teens. MRI scans suggest that both groups often have enlargements of the brain's fluid-filled ventricles and reduced amounts of other brain tissue. These conditions seem to increase with

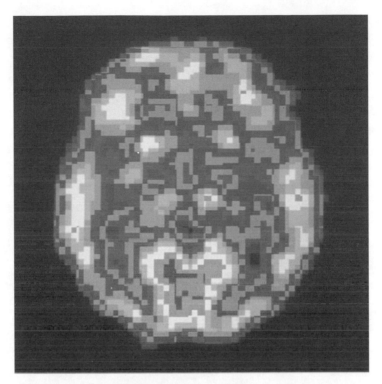

PET scans such as this one of the brain of a schizophrenic patient are becoming a valuable tool in the diagnosis of schizophrenia. With imaging techniques of this kind, researchers can compare a schizophrenic's brain activity with that of a healthy person.

age. It's possible they may begin when a baby is developing in the mother's womb.

On the other hand, another study suggests that the drugs given to treat schizophrenia can themselves affect the brain's structure. In this case, MRI scans show that some areas of the brain used in regulating movement and in thinking increase in size for schizophrenics who use antipsychotic drugs, but not for those who do not use them.

And a study involving PET scans suggests that schizophrenics, who are often forgetful, show a different pattern of brain activity from most people while trying to remember words. Apparently, schizophrenics have more difficulty thinking about the meanings of words while memorizing them. The ultimate significance of this and other findings is still being debated.

own "risk factor" is increased to approximately 3 percent. According to material made available by the British Columbia Schizophrenia Society, if you have a parent, brother, or sister who is schizophrenic, your risk factor is increased to 10 percent. If both your biological parents are schizophrenic, your risk factor may be as high as 40 percent. If you have an identical twin who has the disease, your chance of being affected is also around 40 percent; by contrast, for nonidentical twins, the risk factor is only slightly greater (10 to 15 percent) than that for an ordinary brother or sister.

Although children in the general population have just a 1 percent chance of developing schizophrenia, the identical twin of a child with schizophrenia has a 48 percent chance of developing the illness. Clearly there is some relationship between schizophrenia and a person's genetic makeup.

Does that mean that young people diagnosed as schizophrenic should refrain from marrying and having children? No, but it's important for them to consider the situation thoughtfully. There are two special issues to think about:

- Most parents have to work to support their children. Is the schizophrenic's condition controlled well enough so that he or she can hold down regular employment?

- Raising children can cause great stress to parents because of emotional tensions and increasing monetary costs as the child grows older. How might this kind of added stress affect the schizophrenic's ability to cope with the illness?

There is another important point to remember. It's believed that children do *not* inherit the actual disorder. Rather, what they inherit is a tendency to develop the disorder. Children of schizophrenics seem to be more vulnerable to it than children of non-schizophrenics. Thus, although genetics appears to be a factor, it is not the *cause* of schizophrenia.

Furthermore, investigators aren't sure how schizophrenic tendencies, or predispositions, develop or are transmitted from parent to child. And there is as yet no accurate way to predict whether any given child of a schizophrenic parent will actually develop the disease.

The genetic statistics mentioned above reveal two equally important findings: (1) schizophrenic tendencies may be inherited, but (2) genetics obviously is *not* the complete explanation. For example, we saw that, on the average, for every 10 sets of identical twins among whom one partner has schizophrenia, the other twin will also develop schizophrenia in four cases. But what about the six other cases (more than half) in which the second twin is never stricken by the disease? The implication is that other factors—probably environmental—must be at work.

CHEMICAL IMBALANCES AND OTHER PROBLEMS IN THE BRAIN

So what might be the root cause of schizophrenia? The best research indicates that the individual is afflicted by a chemical imbalance in the brain. This imbalance might result in no extraordinary problems until outside factors bring stress into the person's life, setting off the illness.

Chemical and physical research has focused on many areas:

- **Neurotransmitters:** These are chemical substances that relay impulses between nerves. When they are absent or in short supply, they can cause responses in nerves to be delayed, reduced, or scrambled. In studying neurotransmitters, researchers attempt to understand how they are created and maintained, how they work, and what causes them to function improperly. For many years, neurotransmitters have been suspected as keys to the mystery of schizophrenia and other mental disorders.

- **Blood circulation:** Blood flow within the brain can affect a person's thought processes and ability to think. Does cerebral blood flow differ significantly between schizophrenics and others? So far, this question has no conclusive answer.

- **Structural abnormalities in the brain:** Studies have repeatedly found various structural differences in the brains of people with schizophrenia. The exact meaning of these abnormalities is still being investigated. (See "Exploring Changes in the Brain" in this chapter.)

WHAT TRIGGERS THE SYMPTOMS?

While researchers strive to pinpoint the cause (or causes) of schizophrenia, they're also interested in factors that may stimulate its symptoms. For example, street drugs (marijuana, cocaine, amphetamines, etc.) do not cause the disease. But they can heighten the symptoms in a schizophrenic person and possibly cause relapses during treatment. Doctors urge everyone to avoid street drugs, but the warning is especially urgent for the mentally ill.

Similarly, doctors advise caution with other substances. The occasional consumption of alcohol apparently has little effect on a person's psychotic state, but heavy consumption can be disastrous. In addition to possibly contributing to delusions and other psychotic symptoms, alcohol—a depressant—can be very dangerous when consumed while a person is taking medication, as schizophrenics frequently are. The combination of alcohol with certain tranquilizers, for example, can jeopardize the user's life.

Heavy smoking and excessive coffee drinking also can complicate the life of a schizophrenic because of the drugs (nicotine and caffeine) they introduce into the bloodstream. Even the use of over-the-counter drugs

The death of a loved one is a traumatic event in anyone's life. To a schizophrenic like this man, such an event can bring on a relapse or worsen symptoms that have been under control.

(decongestants, antihistamines) for relief from colds and flu should be considered with great care.

Schizophrenic relapses can also be triggered and their symptoms worsened by factors outside the person's control. Examples include a traumatic event (death of a loved one, loss of a job, etc.), worries over schoolwork, or tension on the job. Young adulthood is an especially stressful period of life. This is the time when most individuals leave home and confront the challenge of making their own way in the world. For the schizophrenic, it can be a hellish period of crisis with no apparent end in sight.

A CONSPIRACY OF CAUSES?

In sum, it seems likely that no single factor can be blamed for schizophrenia. Rather, scientists suspect a sinister combination of culprits: genetics, chemical imbalances, the person's surroundings.

This schizophrenic was forced from his home. Without the support of family and friends, patients have even more difficulty dealing with their illness.

- Though no single gene is known to cause the disorder, genetic composition apparently influences a person's disposition toward schizophrenic tendencies.
- Though no single biochemical deficiency or abnormality can as yet be blamed for sure, such chemical problems almost certainly are in play.

- Though the person's environment may have a role, attempts to define a standard "schizophrenic environment" yield inconsistent findings.

- Though no specific category of stress is suspected, it's almost certain that stress plays a part in the development and worsening of psychotic symptoms.

Why do these various influences come together to disrupt one individual's entire life, when a similar set of circumstances leaves no permanent scar on someone else? The "formula" that produces schizophrenia is still unclear. And there may be many formulas that bring on the same tragic result.

Medication has helped this young man gain control of his psychological troubles. But even with successful medication, most schizophrenics need group or individual counseling to help them cope with their illness.

6

TREATMENT AND CARE

There is as yet no permanent cure for schizophrenia. But most cases of the disease can be treated with medication. Some patients who faithfully follow their treatment seem to shed their schizophrenic symptoms completely. The majority, however, should expect relapses. Even so, most of the difficulties caused by the disease can be overcome.

Of course, the patient must *seek* help before doctors can go to work. One schizophrenic, quoted in Jordan's article, recorded that the moment she realized she needed help was "the moment I started recovering." For years, she had denied being ill; she figured she was "just strange." It wasn't until she realized the problem was much deeper that she could begin the return to a happy life.

MEDICATION

Drugs work differently in different individuals. A drug that seems to help one person overcome a particular schizophrenic symptom may have little effect in another person. Since the causes of schizophrenia are not known, medicating it involves some experimentation. Certain symptoms are more dominant in some patients than in others, so it's obvious that no single "cure-all" exists. Doctors have to adjust levels of medication as they seek the best treatment for a patient. They may have to abandon one drug altogether and try another.

This period of experimenting is usually the hardest for the patient. Even when the right prescription or prescriptions are found, they may have side effects such as restlessness, drowsiness, muscle tightness, appetite change, or blurry eyesight. (Almost all medications can have some unpleasant side effects.) And there may be long-term side effects, such as tardive dyskinesia, a condition that produces uncontrollable, sometimes grotesque movements of the body and face.

Doctors try to determine the best drug and the smallest dosage that will help an individual overcome schizophrenic symptoms. Usually, the more severe the symptoms, the higher the drug dosage required. But if an effective prescription can be identified, it will help reduce the symptoms and lessen the likelihood of their returning.

Several types of medication have been used to treat schizophrenia. Some are pills, others are injected. Since the middle of the 20th century, physicians have relied increasingly on drugs known as antipsychotics. Generally these drugs, also called neuroleptics, work to subdue anxiety and hyperactivity, counteract hallucinations, or reduce aggression. They have helped many schizophrenics distinguish between reality and fantasy, make better decisions, and live more normal lives.

The commonly prescribed antipsychotics include these:

- *Thorazine*, a brand name for chlorpromazine, belongs to a group of drugs known as phenothiazines. Their main effect is to block the action of a neurotransmitter called dopamine.

A number of antipsychotic medications are available, and between 80 and 90 percent of schizophrenics are now helped by drugs. With the most recent medications, the side effects tend to be minor.

First synthesized in the 1950s, chlorpromazine started a revolution in the treatment of schizophrenia. Often, however, chlorpromazine and other phenothiazines have serious side effects.

- *Mellaril* (thioridazine) is another phenothiazine, closely related to Thorazine.

- *Haldol* (haloperidol) is from a group of tranquilizers known as butyrophenones. Besides helping with symptoms of schizophrenia, it is often used to control the facial tics and vocal utterances in Tourette's syndrome.

- *Clozaril* (clozapine), a relatively new medication, is a distant chemical relative of tranquilizers like Valium and Xanax. Clozaril has proved especially valuable in helping patients who fail to respond to other antipsychotics, and for most people it seems to have fewer side effects. In a small number of cases, though, it can cause a sudden and potentially fatal drop in white blood cells, so patients who take it must be monitored carefully.

- *Risperdal* (risperidone), another recent drug, was approved for use in the United States in 1994. It acts on brain receptors for the neurotransmitters dopamine and serotonin. In comparison to most earlier antipsychotics, it appears to work faster and have greater effect on the negative symptoms of schizophrenia like listlessness and flattening of the emotions.

Whatever the medication prescribed, it is usually vital that patients continue to take it regularly. Overall, as many as 80 percent of patients who discontinue their antipsychotic medication suffer relapses of the disease within two years. Only about 40 percent of those who continue taking their medicine have relapses during that period. Those who decide they don't need to continue treatment are initially deceived because their symptoms usually don't recur immediately. And since the unpleasant side effects of the medication go away, they have the false notion that they are better off without treatment.

OTHER MEDICAL TREATMENTS

Researchers are constantly exploring every conceivable way to deal with mental disorders. For some diseases, drugs may not be the only answer.

Although recent medications have proved effective in helping schizophrenics, many health care activists support increased funding for drug research, as at this 1999 rally in Washington, D.C.

Vitamins are necessary ingredients for stable health. Different vitamins are known to provide different benefits to the body. Could there be a vitamin or combination of vitamins that, if administered in high dosages, might help overcome a schizophrenic's chemical imbalance and thus counteract the symptoms of the disease?

Studies have been disappointing, according to the NIMH. Some improvement has been seen in schizophrenic test patients taking high levels of vitamins, but it seems doubtful that improvement can be credited wholly to the vitamins. Other patients on the same megavitamin treatment show no improvement. On another research front, sociomedical studies are trying to determine whether children born to undernourished mothers have uncommonly high rates of schizophrenia.

One dramatic and wrenching form of treatment that has been tried for schizophrenia is electroconvulsive therapy (ECT). This involves connecting electric wires to the patient and quickly passing an electrical shock through his or the forehead. Of course, anesthesia is administered before the surge is given, so the patient isn't hurt by the electricity, but the treatment can produce such unwanted side effects as possible memory loss.

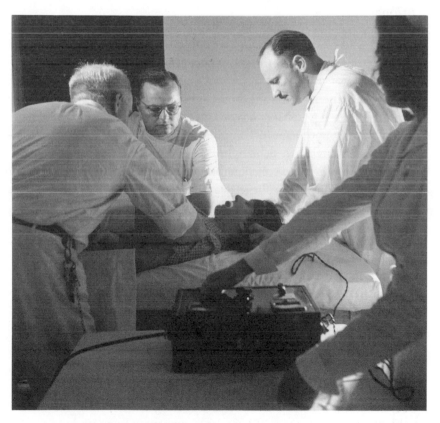

This patient is undergoing ECT (electroconvulsive therapy), also known as shock treatment. Now used only for the most severe cases of depression, shock treatment was once used commonly for schizophrenic patients.

ECT does not permanently cure any psychological disorder, and today it is rarely used in the treatment of schizophrenia. Doctors consider it most often when their psychotic patients are severely depressed—perhaps suicidal—or fail to show improvement after extended efforts to identify helpful medication. In certain instances it can help relieve accompanying symptoms (like depression) that occur during a schizophrenic episode.

A still more radical form of treatment is brain surgery. In rare, severe circumstances of schizophrenia, doctors perform a kind of surgery called a lobotomy. In this procedure they cut into the prefrontal lobe of the cerebrum, the part of the brain that coordinates much of human intelligence. This is a very serious operation that can permanently affect the patient's personality. Today it is rarely even considered in treating schizophrenia.

THERAPY AND REHABILITATION

Medication and other forms of treatment can help restore a normal, peaceful state of mind, but they can't make up for the person's loss of social development. As we've seen, schizophrenia usually comes on when the victim is a teenager or young adult. Those are the years during which we study and begin developing the base of knowledge that will support us through life. Schizophrenia often disrupts this important learning process at the worst possible time. It's very difficult to earn a high school diploma or college degree when the mind is ravaged by delusions and hallucinations.

It is during those same years that young people develop social skills and learn to build lasting relationships. Schizophrenia can make this stage of the emotional growing process all but impossible.

In addition to medication, then, schizophrenics may need psychosocial treatment and therapy as part of their overall plan of care. This kind of treatment comes in many forms, and it may take place in hospitals or at facilities within the community. Unfortunately, some schizophrenia victims live in areas where such care is limited.

PSYCHOTHERAPY AND SUPPORT GROUPS

Psychotherapy usually isn't possible as long as the person is lost in a world of troubled fantasy. When those symptoms are under control, though, psychotherapy can help the person build a normal life.

Individual counseling with a trained therapist can be extremely helpful to a schizo-phrenic. This type of therapy is usually combined with medication and sometimes with group or family therapy.

Therapy may be of several different types:

- **Individual:** This involves one-on-one sessions with a psychi-atrist, social worker, or other mental health worker. The pro-fessional will help the individual probe both past experiences and current feelings, problems, and interactions with others. Gradually, the patient comes to understand his or her illness better. This helps the person see where imaginings differ from reality. This type of "reality orientation" is a key to suc-cessful therapy. Some studies have shown that this personal kind of therapy works best for schizophrenics who live with their families.

- **Family:** Here the therapist involves the person's parents, husband or wife, children, or siblings in the therapy sessions. These meetings can help the family better understand the world of the ill person, while also letting them express how the illness is affecting family relations. Since patients are often released from hospitalization into the care of the family, this type of therapy can be invaluable. Family members are involved in arranging the patient's treatment plan, and they learn of useful services available to help them with home care.

- **Group:** As patients progress in recovering from schizophrenic symptoms, group meetings can reinforce their understanding of the illness. These sessions involve one or more therapists who meet with several patients, perhaps as many as 12, at once. The individuals can learn much from each other as they share insights about their struggles. Hopefully, they can see common patterns of delusions and hallucinations and realize their true nature. Group sessions can help them prepare for life in the outside world.

Schizophrenics can also benefit from self-help groups. These might consist of other schizophrenics who have been treated successfully, as well as relatives of schizophrenics. Sometimes these groups are guided by professionals, but they are not therapy sessions. Rather, they are support groups. If nothing more, they remind the sufferers that they are not alone. Some of these groups also become active in local government issues, pressing for improvements in the treatment facilities of their city or county and making the public aware of biases against individuals with psychological disorders.

In addition to medical treatment, therapy, and family/peer support, schizophrenics can benefit in practical ways from rehabilitation programs. These may provide job counseling and even hands-on training. Participants may learn social skills, along with how to manage their finances. The purpose of an overall care plan is not just to release the people from the hospital and provide effective treatment, but to help them lead happy, productive lives in the outside world.

IS HOSPITALIZATION REQUIRED?

Until a generation ago, most doctors would have said yes. Even today, many schizophrenics have to be hospitalized in order for professionals to bring their symptoms under control and determine the best form of medication. Some patients have to remain hospitalized for long periods of time, and then have to be readmitted occasionally.

For long-term treatment, the general trend in medical care during the 1980s and 1990s has been toward home care and treatment at "out-patient" centers or at short-term residential programs within the person's community. One reason is the rising cost of institutional medical care. Also, doctors know that many long-term patients become dependent on the hospital or other institution and grow increasingly "estranged" from their families and the community. If possible, it's best for persons with psychological disorders to learn to function in normal social and community settings. And, of course, such settings make it easier for sufferers to interact with and get the support of friends and family.

Short-term residential centers provide a place for ill persons to live in a protected, nonstressful environment while they adjust to their medication and begin the process of putting their lives together.

When schizophrenics return to their homes, it's essential that their families participate in the task of healing. The family must not try to deny the illness, but must realize it can be managed—with their help. Parents or spouses should educate themselves about the disease. They should be aware of the community programs and other sources of support available for them and their loved ones. Counseling programs can be informative for the family, as well as being helpful to the patient. Family members must learn to communicate with their ill relative and to cope with the stress the household will face because of the illness.

Teachers of the very young are in a good position to recognize the early warning signs of mental illness. They also serve an important role in teaching children that the mentally ill are not bad or dangerous—stereotypes that the children may have encountered at home or in the media.

THE FUTURE—AND HOW YOU CAN HELP

I n the past quarter century, people suffering from schizophrenia and other mental disorders have been given reason to hope. Their chances of leading useful, happy lives are much better today than they were a generation ago. It is estimated that as many as 25 percent of schizophrenics now recover almost fully, and about 50 percent show at least partial recovery. The remaining 25 percent need long-term help. Those prospects should become even brighter as medical research uncovers more of the mystery and finds more effective ways to combat the disease.

The speed and extent of these advances depend largely on the availability of treatment. Doctors need different kinds of treatment options, since the symptoms vary from patient to patient and different individuals respond differently to any given medication. Schizophrenics also need various kinds of treatment facilities. Patients with severe symptoms require fully equipped hospital wards staffed with psychiatric and medical professionals. Patients with less severe symptoms do not need such an intensive level of care, and for them this environment would be counterproductive. Rather, these recovering individuals need facilities where they can learn social or job skills in an atmosphere that fosters independence.

With regard to research, investigators need funding for a broader range of work. Many different areas of medicine and science can contribute to improved treatment for schizophrenics.

While researchers and doctors work to understand the disease and treat it more effectively, the public and those close to schizophrenic patients can help paint a brighter picture. Better education can lead to the elimination of the harmful prejudice people harbor toward the mentally ill. Individually, friends and loved ones can improve the schizophrenic's life by patiently encouraging him or her along the road to recovery.

HOW THE FAMILY CAN HELP

The schizophrenic's first line of support, apart from professional medical care, is the family. In many ways, great and small, family members can be life savers. Research has shown that a healthy family environment can significantly help bring about stabilization of the ill person's condition and can help decrease the chance of traumatic relapses.

OBSERVING WARNING SIGNALS

Family members are usually the first to observe schizophrenic symptoms. Early warning signals, as described by the British Columbia Schizophrenia Society, might include the following, in various combinations:

- Declining interest in sports, school, or other areas of life in which the person was once keenly involved
- Discontinuation of longtime friendships
- Difficulty concentrating
- Neglect of personal hygiene
- Sleep irregularity
- Poor eating habits and dramatic weight change
- Depression or apparent lack of emotion when certain emotions are natural in given situations
- Inexplicable glee or silliness
- Odd physical expressions and behavior
- Blank stares

Schizophrenics often resist evaluation at first. Family or close friends must take the initiative in addressing the problem and trying to persuade the individual to seek medical help.

FAMILY SUPPORT

Once the person is evaluated, stabilized, and placed on medication, relatives can help ensure that their loved one follows the prescribed treatment. Schizophrenics are often inclined to stop taking their medicine—particularly when the symptoms disappear—and this increases the likelihood of relapse.

Family members can make sure the individual receives balanced meals and regular exercise and rest. Schizophrenia can cause changes in

Schizophrenia can be so overwhelming and disruptive that a patient feels totally out of sync with the world. In this situation family members can play a huge role in helping to stabilize the person's condition.

the patient's eating habits and regular activities. This can be a serious problem if, for example, the sufferer has experienced a delusion of being poisoned and is afraid to eat. Or the medicine prescribed to combat the symptoms of the disease can also cause irregularity in normal health habits. This is true with any psychological disorder.

Relatives can help build the sick person's confidence and encourage independence. However, they must be careful not to pressure the individual. Their goal is to reduce stress, not to create it. They should be careful not to judge or criticize the person's actions or progress.

It is essential that the family provide a structured home environment with familiar, predictable routines. Family members must be consistent in their actions and attitudes when relating to the troubled relative.

Stress can occur after changes in a family's situation, such as relocation, a change in a parent's employment, or a brother or sister moving away from home. These pending developments should be discussed with the patient in advance, thus allowing him or her time to prepare emotionally.

The ill person should be kept relaxed and calm at all times. When tension arises, supporting relatives must control their own emotions.

Caregivers must honor the person's need for privacy, yet be available to discuss problems and gently encourage open communication. Solving problems together helps build an invaluable bond between patient and relatives.

The most important requirement of family and professional caregivers, though, is patience. There is no quick recovery from schizophrenia.

Family members often find it helpful to keep a journal. They might make a record of the different medications that have been tried, as well as the frequency and severity of certain symptoms they observe. By close observation, relatives might be able to detect warning signs before a relapse occurs and to help lessen its effects.

In order to be calm and effective, the caregiver needs to be mindful of his or her own well-being. The relative needs personal time alone and ways to release tension and emotions away from the home. Support groups and confidants are vital for the caregiver. A physically and emotionally healthy relative will be most effective in helping the schizophrenic.

If the loved one is an adult child, living at home may or may not be the best scenario for improvement. Moving out—with the family's full support—can be an important step toward independence. It can also provide valuable "space" for both the patient and the family. The result can be a happier, less stressful family relationship when the family members do come together. However, this is a very delicate decision, one that should be made by the patient without pressure. And if the individual does move out, it's important that he or she feel welcome to return home if independent living doesn't work out.

If the patient remains at home, the family might suggest that the person get out of the house more often and try different activities. Relatives can offer to provide transportation and perhaps accompany the individual on these excursions. Such steps toward independence should be presented gradually. The patient must not feel pressured to show fast progress or to meet difficult goals.

Although it's necessary to treat a schizophrenic child with special care, parents must remember other family members. Not only is there a danger of deep jealousy, but siblings may also harbor fears of contracting the disease themselves.

Having friends who will listen is especially important to a schizophrenic. Just by listening, friends can help a person sort out her problems.

HOW FRIENDS CAN HELP

An understanding friend is invaluable—and all too rare—to a person suffering from schizophrenia. The friend needs to be sympathetic and patient, but realistic.

For example, when the schizophrenic is obviously deluded, the friend must not go along with the fantasy. The best response, rather, is to point out tactfully the difference between what the sufferer perceives and what the friend sees. While assuring the schizophrenic that what he or she is trying to express is understood, the friend should explain that he has a different understanding of the situation.

Friends can perform an important service by helping the individual focus on completing school assignments or maintaining job performance, and they can help normalize the person's eating and sleeping habits. If street drugs or other harmful substances are a threat, friends can gently steer the schizophrenic away from these temptations.

By getting to know the person's family, learning about the disease, and becoming an active member of the support team, friends can serve a unique role in restoring the schizophrenic to health.

HOW TEACHERS CAN HELP

At school, teachers are often in a position to recognize early signals of psychological problems in a student. Such warning signs might include dramatic declines in academic performance, swings in mood between depression and euphoria, inability to concentrate, and listlessness. Thus it is important for teachers to have a basic understanding of the nature of schizophrenia and other mental disorders.

Teachers can help educate students by discussing schizophrenia and other types of mental illness in the classroom. They can go far in stimulating learning about the disorders and in correcting erroneous, sensational opinions about the mentally ill.

With treatment, some students who have been diagnosed as schizophrenics are able to return to school. Teachers can help them progress by encouraging them and working with them to set realistic goals. As with direct caregivers, it's important for teachers to help minimize stress in the student's life. The teacher can urge the student's peers to reach out to their troubled classmate.

A teacher, like no other role model, can instill hope in the individual's mind at a critical point in development.

A QUESTION OF COMMUNITY

Schizophrenia is a tragic disease. Like other kinds of tragedies, it must be acknowledged and dealt with. The sooner work begins, the better off the victims will be.

And the disease doesn't harm only those who contract it. It affects families, friends, and the community at large. By educating yourself about schizophrenia, you can help individuals within your sphere of influence overcome its symptoms and establish a peaceful, organized lifestyle. In this way, you can actively join in the battle against the disorder.

APPENDIX

FOR MORE INFORMATION

Parents of children and adolescents with psychiatric disorders, together with mental health professionals and teachers, have established national organizations that provide education, support, advocacy services, and research facilities. Many of these national groups also have local chapters.

American Academy of Child and Adolescent Psychiatry
3615 Wisconsin Ave., N.W.
Washington, DC 20016
(202) 966-7300

American Medical Association
515 North State St.
Chicago, IL 60610
(312) 464-5000
http://www.ama-assn.org

American Psychiatric Association
1400 K St., N.W.
Washington, DC 20005
(202) 682-6000
http://www.psych.org

American Psychological Association
750 First St., N.E.
Washington, DC 20002
(202) 336-5500
http://www.apa.org

The National Alliance for Research on Schizophrenia and Depression
60 Cutter Mill Rd.
Suite 404
Great Neck, NY 11021
(516) 829-0091
http://www.mhsource.com/narsad.
   html

National Alliance for the Mentally Ill
200 North Glebe Rd.
Suite 1015
Arlington, VA 22203-3754
(703) 524-7600
(800) 950-6264
http://www.nami.org

National Association of Social Workers
750 First St., N.E.
Suite 700
Washington, DC 20002
(202) 408-8600
http://www.naswdc.org

National Institute of Mental Health Information Resources and Inquiries Branch
5600 Fishers Lane
Room 7C-02
Rockville, MD 20857
(301) 443-4513

National Mental Health Association
1021 Prince St.
Alexandria, VA 22314-2971
(703) 684-7722
(800) 969-6942
http://www.nmha.org/index.cfm

**National Mental Health Consumers'
Association**
311 S. Juniper St., Room 902
Philadelphia, PA 19107
(215) 735-2465
http://www.libertynet.org/mha/
chouse/cl_house.html

Schizophrenia Society of Canada
75 The Donway West #814
Don Mills, Ontario M3C 2E9
Canada
Tel (416) 445-8204
Fax (416) 445-2270
http://www.schizophrenia.ca/

World Schizophrenia Fellowship
238 Davenport Rd.
P.O. Box 118
Toronto, Ontario M5R 1J6
Canada
(416) 975-1631, (416) 960-1808
http://www.origo.com/wsf/

APPENDIX

BIBLIOGRAPHY

American Psychiatric Association. *Diagnostic and Statistical Manual of Mental Disorders*, 4th edition. Washington, D.C.: American Psychiatric Press, 1994.

————. *Textbook of Psychopharmacology*. Washington, D.C.: American Psychiatric Press, 1995.

————. *Treatment of Psychiatric Disorders*, 2nd edition. 2 vols. Washington, D.C.: American Psychiatric Press, 1995.

"Antipsychotics and Brain Damage," *Science News* 154, no. 25 (December 19, 1998).

Bernstein, Douglas A., Alison Clarke-Stewart, Edward J. Roy, and Christopher D. Wickens. *Psychology*, 4th edition. Boston: Houghton Mifflin, 1997.

British Columbia Schizophrenia Society. "Schizophrenia: Youth's Greatest Disabler."
(Available at: http://www.mentalhealth.com/book/p40-sc02.html.)

"DNA Links Reported for Schizophrenia," *Science News* 154, no. 10 (September 5, 1998).

"Genetic Hint of Psychosis," *Science News* 153, no. 6 (February 7, 1998).

Harmon, Daniel E. *The Tortured Mind: The Many Faces of Manic Depression*. Philadelphia: Chelsea House Publishers, 1998.

Hyde, Alexander P. *Living with Schizophrenia: A Guide for Patients and Their Families*, 2nd edition. Chicago: Contemporary Books, 1982.

Jordan, J. C. "Schizophrenia—Adrift in an Anchorless Reality," *Schizophrenia Bulletin* 21, No. 3 (1995).

Making Space. "What Is Schizophrenia?" (Available at: http://www.netlink.co.uk/users/carers/Making_Space/whatis.html.)

Marshall, Geraldine. "What Is Schizophrenia?" Pamphlet #1. Toronto, Ont.: World Schizophrenia Fellowship, 1994.
(Available at: http://www. origo.com/wsf/p1.html.)

"Memory's Neural Hit in Schizophrenia," *Science News* 154, no. 4 (July 25, 1998).

NARSAD Research Newsletter. Various articles, 1995–1998. National Alliance for Research on Schizophrenia and Depression, Great Neck, N.Y.
(Available at: http://www.mhsourcc.com/narsad.html.)

O'Brien, Barbara [pseud]. *Operators and Things: The Inner Life of a Schizophrenic.* New York: Ace Books, 1958.

Reilly, Margaret A. *Pharmacology.* Philadelphia: Lippincott-Raven, 1997.

"Repeating DNA Linked to Schizophrenia," *Science News* 152, no. 19 (November 8, 1997).

"Schizophrenia and Suicide." Pamphlet #23. Toronto, Ont.: World Schizophrenia Fellowship, 1996. (Available at: http://www.origo.com/wsf/p23.html.)

"Schizophrenia—Dealing with a Crisis." Pamphlet #15. Toronto, Ont.: World Schizophrenia Fellowship, 1992.
(Available at: http://www.origo. com/wsf/p15.html.)

Shives, Louise R. *Basic Concepts of Psychiatric–Mental Health Nursing,* 4th edition. Philadelphia: Lippincott-Raven, 1998.

Shore, David M., editor. "Schizophrenia: Questions and Answers." DHHS Publication No. (ADM) 86-1457. Rockville, Md.: National Institute of Mental Health, 1990.
(Available at: http://www.nimh.nih.gov/publicat/schizo.htm.)

Smith, Douglas W. *Schizophrenia.* Chicago: Franklin Watts, 1993.

Torrey, E. Fuller. *Surviving Schizophrenia: A Manual for Families, Consumers and Survivors,* 3rd edition. New York: Harper Perennial, 1995.

"U.S. Health Official Puts Schizophrenia Costs at $65 Billion." *The Schizophrenia Homepage*
(Available at: http://www.schizophrenia.com/new/costs1. html.)

Van Reekum, Robert, and J. M. Cleghorn. "Report on the Evidence Supporting a Biological Basis for Schizophrenia." Pamphlet #9. Toronto, Ont.: World Schizophrenia Fellowship, 1992.
(Available at: http://www.origo.com/wsf/p9.html.)

APPENDIX

FURTHER READING

Adamec, Christine, and D. J. Jaffe. *How to Live with a Mentally Ill Person: A Handbook of Day-to-Day Strategies.* New York: John Wiley & Sons, 1996.

American Psychiatric Association. *Diagnostic and Statistical Manual of Mental Disorders,* 4th edition. Washington, D.C.: American Psychiatric Press, 1994.

————. *Textbook of Psychiatry,* 2nd edition. Washington, D.C.: American Psychiatric Press, 1994.

Backlar, Patricia. *The Family Face of Schizophrenia: True Stories of Mental Illness with Practical Advice from America's Leading Experts.* New York: Jeremy P. Tarcher, 1995.

Cantor, Sheila. *Childhood Schizophrenia.* New York: Guilford Press, 1988.

Marsh, Diane T., Rex M. Dickens, and E. Fuller Torrey. *How to Cope with Mental Illness in Your Family: A Self-Care Guide for Siblings, Offspring, and Parents.* New York: Putnam, 1998.

Marsh, Diane T., Rex M. Dickens (contributor), and E. Fuller Torrey. *Troubled Journey: Coming to Terms with the Mental Illness of a Sibling or Parent.* New York: Jeremy P. Tarcher, 1997.

Mueser, Kim, and Kim Tornval Mueser. *Coping with Schizophrenia: A Guide for Families.* Oakland, Calif.: New Harbinger Publications, 1994.

Secunda, Victoria. *When Madness Comes Home: Help and Hope for the Children, Siblings, and Partners of the Mentally Ill.* New York: Hyperion, 1997.

Torrey, E. Fuller. *Surviving Schizophrenia: A Manual for Families, Consumers and Providers,* 3rd edition. New York: Harper Perennial, 1995.

Woolis, Rebecca, and Agnes Hatfield. *When Someone You Love Has a Mental Illness: A Handbook for Family, Friends, and Caregivers.* New York: Jeremy P. Tarcher, 1992.

Wyden, Peter. *Conquering Schizophrenia: A Father, His Son and a Medical Breakthrough.* New York: Knopf, 1998.

APPENDIX

GLOSSARY

Alogia: very short or meaningless responses to questions and statements, as if the person can't translate thoughts into words.

Antipsychotics: a group of drugs often used to treat schizophrenia and other psychotic disorders. Although they are chemically diverse, these drugs typically work by blocking the action of certain neurotransmitters, especially dopamine.

Avolition: a condition of being unable to start or continue goal-directed activities, with little interest in work or social activities.

Catatonia: complete ignoring of surroundings, usually coupled with inappropriate stiffening or loosening of the muscles, but sometimes also with excessive activity and excitement.

Delirium: temporary confusion or uncontrolled emotions.

Delusion: a continuing false belief about yourself and your abilities or about the world around you.

Dementia: loss of mental abilities, especially among the elderly.

Echolalia: the compulsive repetition of a word or phrase spoken by someone else.

Echopraxia: the repetition of a motion made by another.

Electroconvulsive therapy: passing a quick electrical shock through the forehead in an attempt to reorder a patient's thought processes.

Hallucination: a condition in which a person imagines something to be real when it is not, usually involving sight, hearing, or smell.

Hereditary: genetically transmitted from parent to offspring. Although schizophrenia itself is not hereditary, children can inherit a tendency to develop the disorder.

Neurotransmitters: chemical substances that transmit impulses between nerves, suspected by researchers to be keys to schizophrenia and other mental disorders.

Paranoia: an assumption that people around you or the world in general is plotting against you.

Remission: a period during which the symptoms of a disease or disorder are not active.

Syndrome: a collection of symptoms that occur together in a disorder.

APPENDIX

INDEX

Affective flattening, 40
Age, at onset of schizophrenia, 24,
    33, 44, 58
Alogia, 37, 40, 44
Alzheimer's disease, 33
Art and schizophrenia, 29–31
Avolition, 40– 41, 44

Bipolar disorder, 55
Bleuler, Eugen, 26
Brain
    chemical imbalances in, 57, 36,
        44, 55
    structural abnormalities in, 36,
        44, 55, 58, 59–60
    tools to measure activities of, 58
British Columbia Schizophrenia
    Society, 21, 24, 25, 47, 56, 76

Caregivers, 73
    effects of schizophrenia on, 47,
        48–49, 50
    victim supported by, 31, 75–76,
        77–79
Catatonia, 35, 40, 43–44

Dadd, Richard, 30
Delirium, 42
Delusions, 26, 27, 35, 43, 44, 55
    types of, 37–38, 39
Dementia, 42
Dementia praecox, 26, 30
Diagnosis, 35, 36, 37, 42–43
Diagnostic and Statistical Manual of
    Mental Disorders, Fourth Edition

(DSM-IV), 40, 42
    and the causes of schizophrenia,
        55
    and the course of schizophrenia,
        44, 45
    schizophrenia characterized in,
        23, 35–36, 41, 43
DSM-IV. See Diagnostic and Statisti-
    cal Manual of Mental Disorders,
    Fourth Edition

Echolalia, 44
Echopraxia, 44
ECT. See Electroconvulsive therapy
Electroconvulsive therapy (ECT), 69
Ethnicity, 36, 39

Gender, 10, 24, 44
Genetics, 53–56, 57, 61, 62
Grandiosity, 38

Hallucinations, 35, 37, 39, 43, 44
    defined, 26–27
    and medications, 66
Hospitalization, 50, 73
Huntington's disease, 55

Jekyll and Hyde, 23
Jordan, Janice, 21, 25, 65

Kafka, Franz, 30

Lobotomy, 70

Manic depression, 55
Media, 31

Medications, 16, 32, 40, 50, 59, 65–66, 67
Michelangelo, 29
Mood disorder, 45
Morgan, 17–18, 21
Multiple personality disorder, 23, 43

NARSAD. *See* National Alliance for Research on Schizophrenia and Depression
National Alliance for Research on Schizophrenia and Depression (NARSAD), 29, 54
National Institute of Mental Health (NIMH), 50, 58, 68
Nijinsky, Vaslav, 30
NIMH. *See* National Institute of Mental Health

O'Brien, Barbara, 31
Operators and Things (O'Brien), 31

Paranoia, 27, 38, 39, 41, 43
Persecution, 37
Previn, Dory, 31
Psychosis, 35, 42
Psychotic disorders, 42–43

Race, 10
Referential delusion, 39

Schizophrenia
    ailments similar to, 42–43
    case studies of, 13, 14, 15, 16–18, 19–20, 21
    causes of, 53, 54–56, 57, 60, 61, 62–63
    course of, 24, 33, 44, 45, 58
    defined, 35
    early warning signals of, 76, 80
    frequency rate of, 10, 13, 55–56

the future for, 10, 75
    impact on victim's life of, 32, 33
    subtypes of, 35, 41, 43–44
    support for victims of, 75–76, 77–79, 80–81
    symptoms of (*see* Symptoms)
    viewed in early societies, 9, 25–26
"Schizophrenia — Adrift in an Anchorless Reality" (Jordan), 21, 25
Shamans, 26
Society
    impact of schizophrenia on, 13, 50, 51, 73
    schizophrenia viewed by, 9, 31–32, 49–50
Split personality, 23, 43
Stevenson, Robert Louis, 23
Suicide, 10, 21, 27, 28, 31
Surviving Schizophrenia (Torrey), 25
Symptoms, 9, 10, 24, 25, 36–37 (*see also* Delusions; Hallucinations)
    negative, 40, 41
    positive, 37–38, 39–40
    triggers of, 60, 61

Therapy, 50, 69–70, 71, 72
Torrey, E. Fuller, 25
Treatment, 10, 33, 50, 67–69, 71, 75 (*see also* Hospitalization; Medications; Therapy)

Ustyugov, Gemady, 31

van Gogh, Vincent, 29, 30
Violence, 32, 50
Vitamins, 68–69

Wain, Louis, 30–31

APPENDIX

PICTURE CREDITS

page

8: Marburg/Art Resource, New York

12: © Alain Dex/Publiphoto/Photo Researchers

14: © Sheila Terry/Science Photo Library/Photo Researchers

16: AP/Wide World Photos

19: AP/Wide World Photos

20: © Shirley Zeiberg Photography

22: © Louise Williams/Science Photo Library/Photo Researchers

24: Oscar Burriel/Latin Stock/Science Photo Library/Photo Researchers

28: AP/Wide World Photos/Richard Drew

29: Giraudon/Art Resource, New York

30: Archive Photos

33: Oscar Burriel/Science Photo Library/Photo Researchers

35: Oscar Burriel/Latin Stock/Science Photo Library/Photo Researchers

36: John Bavosi/Science Photo Library/Photo Researchers

38: AP/Wide World Photos/Steven Senne

41: Oscar Burriel/Science Photo Library/Photo Researchers

45: © Ex-Rouchon/Photo Reserachers

46: © Arthur Tress/Photo Researchers

48: © James Prince/Photo Researchers

51: © 1993 Joseph Sohm/Chromosohm/Photo Researchers

52: Nimatallah/Art Resource, New York

54: Klaus Guldbrandsen/Science Photo Library/Photo Researchers

56: © Shirlery Zeiberg Photography

59: © Hank Morgan/SS/Photo Researcher

61: AP/Wide World Photos

62: © 1988 Laima Druskis/Photo Researchers

64: © Michael Hart 1996/FPG International LLC

66: Food and Drug Administration/Science Photo Library/Photo Researchers

68: Archive Photos

71: AP/Wide World Photos

72: © Jeff Kaufman 1988/FPG International LLC

74: Urban Archives, Philadelphia

77: © Bill Longcore/Photo Researchers

79: PhotoDisc Vol. 45 #45091

Senior Consulting Editor Carol C. Nadelson, M.D., is president and chief executive officer of the American Psychiatric Press, Inc., staff physician at Cambridge Hospital, and Clinical Professor of Psychiatry at Harvard Medical School. In addition to her work with the American Psychiatric Association, which she served as vice president in 1981–83 and president in 1985–86, Dr. Nadelson has been actively involved in other major psychiatric organizations, including the Group for the Advancement of Psychiatry, the American College of Psychiatrists, the Association for Academic Psychiatry, the American Association of Directors of Psychiatric Residency Training Programs, the American Psychosomatic Society, and the American College of Mental Health Administrators. In addition, she has been a consultant to the Psychiatric Education Branch of the National Institute of Mental Health and has served on the editorial boards of several journals. Doctor Nadelson has received many awards, including the Gold Medal Award for significant and ongoing contributions in the field of psychiatry, the Elizabeth Blackwell Award for contributions to the causes of women in medicine, and the Distinguished Service Award from the American College of Psychiatrists for outstanding achievements and leadership in the field of psychiatry.

Consulting Editor Claire E. Reinburg, M.A., is editorial director of the American Psychiatric Press, Inc., which publishes about 60 new books and six journals a year. She is a graduate of Georgetown University in Washington, D.C., where she earned bachelor of arts and master of arts degrees in English. She is a member of the Council of Biology Editors, the Women's National Book Association, the Society for Scholarly Publishing, and Washington Book Publishers.

Daniel E. Harmon is an editor and writer living in Spartanburg, South Carolina. The author of several books on humor and history, he has contributed historical and cultural articles to the *New York Times, Music Journal, Nautilus,* and many other periodicals. He is the managing editor of *Sandlapper: The Magazine of South Carolina* and is editor of *The Lawyer's PC* newsletter. His books in the Chelsea House ENCYCLOPEDIA OF PSYCHOLOGICAL DISORDERS series include *Anorexia Nervosa: Starving for Attention, Life Out of Focus: Alzheimer's Disease and Related Disorders,* and *The Tortured Mind: The Many Faces of Manic Depression.*